GEO

QUICKIE DIVORCE

Linda H. Connell
Attorney at Law

SPHINX® PUBLISHING
AN IMPRINT OF SOURCEBOOKS, INC.®
NAPERVILLE, ILLINOIS
www.SphinxLegal.com

First Edition: 2007

Published by: **Sphinx® Publishing, An Imprint of Sourcebooks, Inc.®**

<u>Naperville Office</u>
P.O. Box 4410
Naperville, Illinois 60567-4410
630-961-3900
Fax: 630-961-2168
www.sourcebooks.com
www.SphinxLegal.com

This publication is designed to provide accurate and authoritative information in regard to the subject matter covered. It is sold with the understanding that the publisher is not engaged in rendering legal, accounting, or other professional service. If legal advice or other expert assistance is required, the services of a competent professional person should be sought.

From a Declaration of Principles Jointly Adopted by a Committee of the American Bar Association and a Committee of Publishers and Associations

This product is not a substitute for legal advice.

Disclaimer required by Texas statutes.

Library of Congress Cataloging-in-Publication Data

Connell, Linda H.
  Quickie divorce : everything you need to save time, money, and get it done fast and legally / by Linda H. Connell. -- 1st ed.
     p. cm.
  Includes index.
  ISBN-13: 978-1-57248-606-5 (pbk. : alk. paper)
  ISBN-10: 1-57248-606-6 (pbk. : alk. paper)
  1. Divorce suits--United States--Popular works. I. Title.

KF535.Z9C66 2007
346.7301'66--dc22
                                                                2007015206

Printed and bound in the United States of America.
SB — 10 9 8 7 6 5 4 3 2 1

Contents

Introduction

This book is meant to assist people who either are considering filing for divorce or have been served with a divorce petition, and who wish to speed the process along in order to move on. There is a difference, however, between obtaining a *quick* divorce and making a *hasty* decision as to whether to divorce. Getting that final divorce decree in a prompt manner may seem to be a good idea, but it is important that you do not take the decision to pursue divorce lightly. There are other possible options, which are discussed in Chapter 1.

Once you have concluded that divorce is the best way to proceed, you will need to determine whether you should retain an attorney to represent you. Some of the issues pertaining to finding and hiring a lawyer are covered in Chapter 2. Please note that no book can take the place of the advice of an attorney who is familiar with the individual set of facts at hand. If you choose to represent yourself (known as proceeding *pro se*), it is important to know how to find the legal principles that will support your case and the procedural rules that you must follow in order to present your side. Legal research techniques are discussed in Chapter 3.

A general walk-through of a divorce case takes place in Chapter 4. Pleadings, discovery of information, and the hearing itself are covered. In

Chapter 5, possible *grounds* for divorce, or the basis upon which the divorce is requested, are discussed. The topics of *no-fault divorce,* which loosens the grounds requirement, and *covenant marriage,* which limits the available grounds for divorce in certain states, are included. Residency requirements, which may lengthen or shorten the divorce procedure depending upon the state, are the subject of Chapter 6. Chapter 7 discusses divorces that are obtained from sister states and foreign countries. Such divorces can sharply reduce the length of time from filing to final divorce decree, but the parties must take care to understand whether their own home states will recognize and honor the divorce.

Summary proceedings and uncontested divorces, which typically dispense with many of the steps involved in contested divorce cases, are dealt with in Chapter 8. An uncontested divorce can result from one party failing to show up at court in the case, but more likely, it will come from the parties agreeing to a settlement of all issues before the matter actually goes before a judge.

The most likely causes of disagreement in divorce cases are: the *property settlement,* which is the division of assets and debts from the marriage; *maintenance* issues, also known as alimony; and questions regarding *child custody, support, and visitation.* Overviews of these topics are found in Chapters 9, 10, and 11. Chapter 12 provides guidance for emergency cases, in which immediate steps are necessary to protect oneself or one's children or property from the actions of the other spouse.

Chapters 13 and 14 discuss the post-decree issues of enforcement, modification, and termination of divorce-related court rulings. The divorce decree is a judicial order, and there can be legal consequences for those who do not obey its terms. Even after the judge has issued a final decree, the terms of the order may be changed under certain circumstances. In some instances, one or both parties can ask that terms of the order be terminated. An example is when the judge ends one spouse's obligation to pay alimony when the other spouse remarries.

Finally, appendices found at the end of the book will provide state-specific information on the topics covered in this book, blank forms to assist in preparing court documents that may be necessary in a divorce case, and other resources if you need additional information.

Gender references found herein are determined solely for purposes of clarity. *Spouse* can refer to either males or females. The terms *divorce* and *dissolution* are used interchangeably.

Is a Quick Divorce Right for You?

If you have researched your options and have determined that divorce is the best one, you must decide whether it is in your best interest to go through the process quickly or not. Keep in mind that certain circumstances may make it wiser to actually slow down the progress of your case. If you have reason to believe that your chances for a favorable divorce settlement will improve over time, then a speedy divorce clearly is not for you.

To illustrate, consider the example of a spouse's overtime hours.

EXAMPLE:

Steve and Peggy are having marital difficulties, and each is contemplating divorce. Steve begins to take on extra hours at work. He does this in part because he sees problems in the marriage and believes it is in his best interest to have some cash saved in case he needs to get his own lawyer. His other reason for working overtime is that he wishes to avoid the stress of being at home, where the environment is less than friendly. Months pass where Steve has taken all the overtime shifts he can get his hands on. Eventually, he can no longer tolerate the situation at home and files for divorce. Peggy asks the judge to order Steve to pay *maintenance*, or *alimony*, as well as child support, based on Steve's take-home pay—including the overtime. If Peggy had filed her own divorce action when Steve began working overtime, the court likely would not have included the extra pay in calculating Steve's maintenance and child support obligations, which are based partly on salary in most states. However, because Steve has established a pattern over time of bringing in a good share of overtime pay, the court rules that the extra money can be considered in determining Steve's liability.

There are certain property interests that you may be entitled to if you are married at the time the interests vest, which may make it worth your while to wait before filing for divorce.

EXAMPLE:

Peggy has a relative, Aunt Sue, who is planning on leaving a large sum of money in her will to "Peggy and her spouse, if she be married at the time of my death." If Aunt Sue is 45 and in good health, it probably will not be worth it for Steve to sit around and wait in a bad marriage for that inheritance. On the other hand, if the payout is high enough or Aunt Sue is in her nineties and in poor health, he just might want to wait after all.

Is a Quick Divorce Possible?

Even if you are sure that you want a divorce and you want it now, there is no guarantee that you will get your wish. As in any legal proceeding, the wheels may turn slower than you would like. Although *no-fault* divorce is an option in many cases, it does not mean that the case will be open and shut. Property disputes, even over items of little value, can turn a simple and otherwise amicable split into a fight to the bitter end. Motions, hearings on ancillary matters, and court date continuances can drag out the proceedings even more.

With almost any divorce involving children, most states have put procedural requirements in place to protect the interests of the kids, particularly in a case where the parents cannot resolve custody and visitation issues on their own. A *custody evaluation*, for example, is an assessment of an entire family, performed by psychologists or other professionals, in order to determine the best living situation for the child. This evaluation can take several months to complete.

The bottom line is that a fast divorce is possible, but only if both parties want a *quickie divorce*.

Speeding Up Your Divorce

So you want a divorce sooner rather than later. Unfortunately, this is only partly within your control. The following chapters will provide you with tips on how to accelerate your case. In the end, however, your own attitude and conduct will have the greatest impact on how quickly you are able to achieve the outcome you desire. Cooperation with both your own attorney and your soon-to-be ex will help move the case along. Of course, that is not to say that you should allow your spouse to walk all over you just so that you can obtain the divorce decree. There may be times when it will be necessary, for your own or your children's best interests, to take a stand against your spouse—even if it throws a monkey wrench into the divorce. The key is to pick your fights wisely; if it is not worth the delay, avoid digging in your heels on every issue. Winning the battle at the expense of shortening the war may not be good strategy.

Even more than having a procedural advantage, such as a home state with a shortened residency requirement, working in partnership with your attorney will hasten the end of your divorce case. It is really just a matter of common sense. Return your attorney's telephone calls. If your attorney tells you to provide information in response to a discovery request, like bank statements or tax returns, get copies of the documents to him or her as quickly as possible.

It is in dealing with your spouse and his or her lawyer that things can get tricky. Here is where your own conduct can go a long way toward speeding up the resolution of your case. Be honest with yourself as to what you truly want out of your divorce, whether it is marital property, maintenance or child support payments, or terms of child custody. Chances are, if you and your spouse are reasonable and can give and take on these matters, you both may be able to reach a marital settlement agreement. This will go further than any time-saving strategy to get you your divorce decree quickly.

◆◆◆

If you do not take the advice in Chapter 2 and hire an attorney to guide you through the dissolution of marriage procedure, here is one more caveat for you. This book is not state-specific but instead gives an overview of the law from a general perspective. Please keep in mind that when referring to this book, there may be statutes in your state that differ from the typical laws on a certain issue. Be sure to check the divorce statutes in your state before proceeding with any kind of legal action regarding your marriage.

CHAPTER 1:
Alternatives to Divorce

If you are considering whether to pursue a divorce, or if your spouse has made the decision for you by having you served with divorce papers, it still is important for you to be aware of the options that may be available to you. Although you may wish to complete the process as quickly as possible, trying to decide the best way to proceed at the outset may save you time in the long run. If you wish to have your marriage *annulled* (declared invalid), you are better off commencing appropriate proceedings right away, rather than going through the entire divorce process first and then deciding annulment is the way to go.

Counseling

Why discuss marital counseling in a book about quick divorce? If the best outcome for you is to *avoid* ending your marriage, that obviously is a better solution than going through all the time and expense of achieving a result that you do not really want.

Marriage counseling is a type of family therapy whereby a qualified mental health professional works with a couple on their relationship. This is different from individual therapy, which focuses on the individual. Couples therapists can serve as objective observers, and can also assist a couple with marital problems by teaching them how to resolve conflicts on their own by working out issues in a constructive manner.

The *American Association for Marriage and Family Therapy* (AAMFT), a professional association representing marriage counselors, is a good resource for additional information about couples therapy. If you have unsuccessfully attempted to convince your spouse to seek marital counseling, the AAMFT suggests that it may be beneficial for you to go by yourself. The AAMFT website, **www.aamft.org**, also can help you to locate a qualified marriage therapist in your area.

Legal Separation

Legal separation is another option that may render divorce unnecessary, which will save you both time and money.

Legal separation describes a situation in which the couple formally lives apart, usually with a court order in place that governs issues like custody and visitation, spousal support, and even division of marital assets, although these often are only temporary orders. The court's final order on these issues generally is not handed down unless and until one of the parties actually files for divorce.

There are a number of reasons a couple would undertake a legal separation. One main reason for separating is to try living apart on a trial basis. Another motive for separating might be that one or both of the parties does not believe in divorce on religious grounds. Others may separate rather than divorce because of financial considerations. For example, staying married a while longer may give one spouse enough time to become vested in a financial interest belonging to the other spouse.

It is important to keep in mind that, in many cases, the arrangements that are made during a separation for issues such as custody and maintenance end up being the final arrangements the court orders if the matter eventually goes on to become a divorce action.

Annulment

An *annulment* is a declaration that a marriage is invalid. The practical effect is to end the marriage, the same as with a divorce. In a number of cases, the grounds for both divorce and annulment overlap. The legal effect, however, is entirely different. A divorce dissolves a valid marriage, while an annulment makes the marriage null and void from the beginning.

In cases of bigamy or where the parties are closely related, no marriage ever existed in the first place. This is the case even if both parties wished to continue the marriage. Legally, it is not even necessary to petition the court for an annulment, since there is no marriage to declare invalid. However, it is a good idea to seek a court order in any event, so that there is documentation of the invalidity.

Other bases for annulment depend on the law of the state in which the annulment is sought. Some of the other grounds to annul a marriage might include:

- insanity;
- consent to marriage obtained by fraud, force, or duress;
- impotence; or,
- minority (underage) of one of the parties.

Other possible grounds for annulment, similar to grounds for divorce, are discussed in Chapter 5.

These other cases, in which annulment must be sought from a court, are called *voidable marriages*. This means the invalidity is not automatic. In some cases, the grounds for annulment might be rendered unavailable. If the petitioning spouse knew of the reason the marriage was voidable and remained in the marriage anyway, he or she might be unable to claim the ground for annulment. For example, if the husband was impotent at the time of the marriage, and the wife either knew of the condition or found out about it later and continued to cohabit with the husband, she might be barred from claiming the impotence as grounds for having the marriage annulled.

When an annulment is granted, most states provide that any children of the marriage are not made illegitimate as a result of the invalidity of the marriage. Custody and support determinations in such a case are similar to those in divorce cases. These issues are discussed further in Chapters 9, 10, and 11.

An annulment is usually harder to get than divorce because, unlike divorce, there is no option of no-fault. This means that the party seeking annulment must provide proof of the grounds. For this reason, it may end up being a more time-consuming process than simply filing for a divorce. If you are looking for a rapid end to a marriage, you might want to go with the divorce. However, some people are set on obtaining an annulment, often for religious reasons; that is, they wish to remarry according to their religious beliefs, and need to have a prior marriage declared invalid before their faith allows them to embark upon another.

CHAPTER 2: Hiring a Lawyer

A person contemplating divorce may be concerned about expenses. It is tempting to try to cut costs by passing up professional legal help in favor of representing oneself in these proceedings. Maybe that is one of the reasons you are reading this book. Unfortunately, while this book provides a lot of useful information, a book cannot replace the individualized advice a competent attorney can provide after reviewing the particular facts of your case.

Pros and Cons

The main disadvantage of hiring an attorney is the cost. However, the advantages almost always make the cost worth it.

The main advantage of working with an attorney is that he or she is likely to have the experience necessary to achieve the best possible outcome for you. Therefore, he or she should be the best source of advice for your particular situation. Almost as important, he or she can be something of an impartial third party, who can give you objective opinions as to your likelihood of success in the various issues concerning your legal case.

Another real plus to having an attorney represent you is the assistance you will have navigating the legal system. Divorce, separation, annulment, and custody cases are loaded with procedural rules and technical requirements. Filing deadlines are easy to miss. Parties may have to draft documents according to very precise pleading requirements before a court will consider the pleadings. Rules may even be different from county to county within your state. Attorneys, especially those who routinely practice in family law courts, usually will already have documents and deadlines programmed into their office computers, and will almost certainly know what other hoops need to be jumped through. Even if there is a procedural area with which a lawyer is unfamiliar, he or she will generally know where to find the information with much greater ease than a nonlawyer.

While unfortunate, it also may be true that a litigant in a divorce action will be taken more seriously if he or she has retained an attorney than if he or she proceeds *pro se*. Even in the case of a judge who gives some leeway to a party representing him- or herself, the other side is entitled to have the *pro se* opponent held to the same court rules as everybody else. However, the reality of the situation is that judges sometimes have less patience for *pro se* litigants, who may not be familiar with procedural rules, filing requirements, or even proper courtroom decorum. For these reasons, retaining a legal professional to handle your case may be the best way to quickly reach a satisfactory result for yourself.

Finding a Lawyer

If you have decided to retain an attorney to represent you, the next step is to locate a capable one. If you do not have a family law attorney already, several resources exist to help you find one.

Lawyer Referral Services

Most states, and often the counties within each state, have professional organizations known as *bar associations*. Many state and local bar associations offer lawyer referral services that an individual may contact and receive the names of area attorneys that practice family law. The individual then must contact the attorney of his or her choice to set up an initial consultation. The consultation typically will take about a half hour, and there usually is a nominal charge, around $20 or $30, regardless of which attorney you consult from the referral service. Appendix A provides listings for various local and state bar association referral services.

Legal Directories

Your local library, as well as the law library in your county courthouse, should have copies of state, regional, and national directories listing most of the attorneys practicing law in the geographical area the directory covers. A number of these directories are available online as well. Martindale-Hubbell and the West Legal Directory are the two main national directories. You can browse their websites at **www.lawyers.com** (Martindale-Hubbell) and **www.lawyers.findlaw.com** (West).

Word of Mouth

Another good way to find a lawyer concentrating in divorce law is to get a referral from a friend who has been through the process and was satisfied with the representation he or she received. Most people know a number of others who have found themselves in divorce court. You can benefit from the experience of someone else who has already had to locate a divorce lawyer.

Attorney and Court Personnel Referrals

You may find that people working regularly in the local courthouse are a good source of referrals. A lawyer you may have used for a different matter in the past might give you a lead on a good family law attorney. If you are in the law library looking through a legal directory, you might try striking up a conversation with the law librarian. He or she interacts with a number of attorneys on a daily basis, and may feel comfortable recommending several to contact.

Advertisements

Many attorneys advertise in publications, on television or radio, in the Yellow Pages, or online. The downside of choosing an attorney from an advertisement is that you may have very little information about your prospective counsel. Most ads will give you some insight into the areas of law in which the lawyer practices, but you may not have much else to go on. You may have to contact the lawyer you are considering by phone and ask for information on the lawyer's educational background and the number of years he or she has practiced family law. This may help you to get a sense of whether or not this particular attorney will be a good representative of your interests.

Consultation

Once you have located an attorney, the next step is to contact his or her office to schedule an initial consultation. This is an opportunity to meet with the attorney and provide him or her with the facts of your case. This is also the time to discuss the lawyer's credentials, experience, and representational style. Generally, initial consultations are brief, especially if you are receiving the consultation at a discounted rate.

Attorney's Representational Style

The lawyer's demeanor and courtroom manner are very important considerations because you should feel comfortable with the attorney's professional approach. Does the lawyer come across as agreeable or combative? Does he or she seem to feel that you should work for settlement of your case, or does he or she seem to want to mount an all-out battle with your spouse? Which of those strategies appeals to you? If you do not agree with his or her litigation methods and demeanor, you should continue your search for another attorney.

Attorney's Fees

Your initial consultation should also include a discussion of attorney's fees. A divorce case, whether speedy or not, can be a very expensive proposition. Attorneys handling these matters generally charge a per-hour fee for all services rendered. Oftentimes, an attorney will have a multileveled fee structure in which he or she will charge one rate for office work and a higher per-hour rate for time spent in court.

A lawyer usually will require a new client to pay a *retainer*, a lump-sum advance payment to cover initial costs and attorney's fees for a certain amount of time. The lawyer deducts his or her fees from the retainer. When the retainer has been spent, he or she will bill you, typically on a monthly basis, for any additional fees.

Attorneys also may pay court costs on behalf of a client and then include the advanced charges on the client's bill. This happens, for example, when the office of the *clerk of court*, where documents in lawsuits are filed, charges a $20 filing fee. The attorney will pay the filing fee from a special account the attorney holds for such a purpose, and then will add the charge to the client's monthly bill for services rendered.

Be sure that the fee agreement that you reach with your lawyer is in writing and signed by you both. Some states even require that attorney-client fee contracts contain certain language before an attorney will be allowed to sue the client for unpaid attorney's fees.

You also should be sure that you understand the attorney's billing policy before you agree to the representation. Ask how often you will be billed, and ask for an estimate of monthly fees. Be suspicious of any attorney who tells you that you have an open-and-shut case that will not require a substantial expenditure of fees. Unless you are filing a petition for dissolution jointly with your spouse, with no issues left to be determined, fees are likely to mount. Also, ask for an itemized bill, with billable hours broken down so that you can see how many hours were spent on each activity. An example of what such a bill might look like appears on page 10.

LAW OFFICES OF GEORGE A. REPP
Attorney at Law
567 Business Street
Springfield, ED 60500
101-555-4567

Samuel Spouse
123 Main Street
Springfield, ED 60500

PERSONAL AND CONFIDENTIAL

April 15, 2007
Client number 07-876

	Hours	Amount
3/20/07: Met with client and prepared Petition for Dissolution of Marriage	1.50	$225.00
3/21/07: Prepared letter and service instructions on Respondent	.50	$75.00
For professional services rendered	2.00	$300.00
3/21/07: Photocopies (32)		$4.80
3/22/07: Clerk of Court; filing fee for Petition for Dissolution		$100.00
Total costs		$104.80
Total amount of this bill:		$404.80
3/31/07: Disbursement from retainer	($404.80)	
Balance due:		$0.00

Please write your reference number on your check when mailing your payment.
Thank you.

Confidentiality

Each state has enacted a code of professional responsibility, which is a set of legal ethical rules to which attorneys are held. Among the most important of these rules is that of *confidentiality*. This means that anything you discuss with your attorney relating to your divorce case will remain between you and your attorney. This is true even with regard to an attorney with whom you have met only once. His or her office staff is held to confidentiality rules as well.

It is in your best interest to be forthright and completely honest with your attorney. It is essential that you provide all of the information he or she asks you for, even if you believe it is insignificant or if you fear that the information will hurt your case. It is better that he or she is aware of any negative information impacting your case than to have it come out during a deposition or, worse, in the middle of court, and to have your attorney be unprepared. This would be a much more difficult situation to remedy than if your lawyer knew of the information well ahead of time and was able to counteract any negative effect.

The Attorney/Client Relationship

If for some reason you do not "click" with the first attorney you meet with, or if you are unable to agree on the terms of your representation, do not be too concerned. A great number of attorneys practice family law, and finding another one should not be a problem. In fact, even if you like the first attorney you contact, it is not a bad idea to consult with more than one, if time and finances allow. Speaking with a second or third attorney may give you a more accurate picture of your chances of success in your case. It also will give you the opportunity to find the lawyer who will best represent your interests.

The type of relationship you have with your lawyer can have a great impact on the result of your case. If it is a successful relationship, you will feel free to discuss any concerns you have about the case, including your lawyer's handling of the matter. You should be comfortable asking questions about all aspects of the representation. Your lawyer should be open to constructive criticism, and also should be willing to explain the legal issues as well as the procedural steps he or she is planning to take. Similarly, your attorney should be satisfied that you are providing him or her with complete and truthful information about the facts of the case, so that he or she is fully prepared to present your side in court.

If you do not feel that you and your attorney have this type of relationship and you are intimidated by him or her, are afraid to ask questions, or do not receive satisfactory answers, then you may want to consider looking for a new attorney.

Even if you are entirely certain that you need to get through your divorce as soon as possible, it is impossible to overstate the importance of taking the time to secure the best representation you can possibly find. No amount of time saved will make it worth having an unsatisfactory result in your case. You may regret retaining the wrong lawyer, if you end up with an unfavorable property settlement or a visitation schedule with which you are not happy, all because you were not compatible or able to communicate effectively with the attorney you settled on.

Hiring Part-Time Legal Help

You may find yourself caught between the desire to obtain a divorce quickly and the need to cut costs in achieving your goal. Hiring a lawyer to help you take care of the matters you cannot handle yourself may be an alternative worth pursuing. Some attorneys might be willing to help you with drafting documents and preparing you for court hearings, while allowing you to do your own filing and other legwork. This may reduce the number of attorney billable hours for which you are charged, without leaving you totally on your own with regard to the legal issues. Not all attorneys are willing to work on a part-time basis, however. Because of ethical requirements that a lawyer do his or her best for a client, some will have qualms about only "partially" representing you.

A recent trend is that of businesses staffed by nonlawyers that provide legal services such as document preparation or other assistance for individuals attempting do-it-yourself legal work. Be wary of such organizations. Lawyers are held to strict rules of professional responsibility to their clients; nonlawyers are not regulated in the same manner. In fact, depending on the services provided, these businesses may even be operating unlawfully.

Nonlawyers are legally prohibited from what is known as the *unauthorized practice of law*. That means that someone who is not a licensed attorney may not give legal advice to another and may not appear in court or enter into negotiations on behalf of another. In many states, preparation of legal documents is also considered practicing law; however, in some states, nonlawyers with paralegal training may be allowed to perform this task. Because state laws differ in this area, you should check the rules in your jurisdiction before retaining a nonlawyer to do any work on your case.

CHAPTER 3:
Finding the Relevant Law

By now you should understand how important it is to have an attorney in a divorce case. However, if you decide to go it alone, or if you have a lawyer and simply want to better understand what is happening in the case, you need to know how to perform legal research. Legal research is how you find the law that applies to your case in order to help you make the best argument. Knowing the law also will help you to decide what position is best for you to take. It is beneficial for you to know whether you can afford to dig your heels in on a particular issue or whether you would be better off being flexible. For example, say that you are in the middle of a divorce and want sole custody of your children. Also say that the law in your state encourages joint custody in most divorce cases. Under the circumstances, if the law does not indicate that you would be entitled to sole custody, you could save much time, effort, and money by adopting a position that is more in line with what the law provides.

To find the relevant law, most of what you need can be found in the law library and on the Internet. Comprehensive law libraries often can be found in the courthouses of most counties and on the campuses of law schools. These libraries usually are open to the public, although you may not be allowed to check out materials, meaning you will have to do all of your research in the library itself. For that reason, the Internet can be a better alternative. Online materials can be downloaded at your convenience, in the privacy of your own home or at your public library. Moreover, Internet sources can provide a lot of additional information that interprets the many cases and statutes that may apply to your case.

However, keep in mind the downside of the Internet: the information that is sent out into cyberspace is largely unregulated and there is no guarantee that the sources are accurate. If you do online research, stick to websites affiliated with reputable organizations, such as the American Bar Association, or law school sites. Companies such as West and Lexis-Nexis offer legal research materials online, for a fee, that are fairly comprehensive. However, these services are expensive for the nonlawyer. Appendix A contains a list of Internet sources that may be of assistance to you in your legal research.

Those who perform legal research often use the terms *primary source* and *secondary source* to describe the various materials they use to support their clients' cases.

Primary Sources

Primary sources of law are comprised of the actual statutes, ordinances, and regulations that have been enacted by federal, state, and local legislative bodies. They also include judicial opinions, known as *case law*, that have been handed down by judges who interpret the legislation. Primary sources are the best places to find the law supporting your particular position, because statutes and case law are the most compelling statements of what the law actually is.

Statutory Codes

Each state has its own *statutory code*, or set of laws enacted by the state legislature that apply to a number of subjects. Other topics may be subject to the power of the U.S. government through Congress. Generally, though, marriage and divorce issues are left to the individual states to regulate. Therefore, if you are researching divorce law for a case that is taking place in your state, you will have to be sure you are looking at the right statutory code for the state. Appendix B provides state-by-state information on divorce law, including the correct statutory citation for each of the fifty states and the District of Columbia.

A *citation* is an abbreviation that makes it easier to find a particular law within a state code. For example, the Illinois Marriage and Dissolution of Marriage Act is found in Chapter 750, Act 5 of the Illinois Compiled Statutes, which is abbreviated as 750 ILCS 5. The section of the Illinois Marriage and Dissolution of Marriage Act that deals with visitation is in Section 607 of the Act. This section would be cited as: 750 ILCS 5/607. To find this provision in the statute, which is extensive, first look for the chapter (Chapter 750). Once you locate the chapter, find Act 5, then Section 607. These provisions should be cited in the standard form throughout the search materials you are using. Some statutes also come in an *annotated* form, which means that each statutory provision includes citations to actual court decisions that relied on that particular section of the statute in reaching a decision.

Case Reporters

When a judge hands down a ruling in a particular case, he or she relies on both statutory law and earlier court opinions from other judges. An attorney will refer to earlier decisions when arguing a case. If the decisions are favorable to the argument the attorney wants to make, he or she will point out to the judge how the legal ruling should be similar because the facts are similar. If, on the other hand, the prior opinions go against the attorney's case, he or she will attempt to point out the differences between the present case and the earlier ones. Previous case law is known as *precedent*. When you are doing your own research, you will need to review the precedent for the issue you are researching to see if the law is favorable or unfavorable to your case.

Judicial opinions are found in published volumes called *case reporters*. Some case reporters contain the appellate and supreme court case opinions for a particular state. Others are regional reporters, and hold opinions for several states in one series. Still others report only federal court cases. Citations to cases found in these reporters have a standard form: the case name (which is made up of the names of the parties to the lawsuit), the volume number of the reporter, the standard abbreviation used for the particular reporter, the relevant page number, and the year of the decision. An example of this standard form of citation is *In re Marriage of Fowler*, 554 N.E.2d 240 (1989). This 1989 opinion appears in Volume 554 of the North Eastern Reporter, Second Series, and begins at page 240.

It is important to note that usually only state appellate and supreme court opinions are published in case reporters. Trial court opinions generally are not published and do not make good precedent.

Secondary Sources

Secondary sources are those that have been made to explain statutory and case law or to categorize the law by topic. Judges and attorneys may look to these sources for help to understand the law in a certain area. Keep in mind, though, that they are not as strongly supportive of a particular legal argument as a primary source would be. Even so, they are great to use as a reference if you do not understand something. Some examples of secondary sources are digests and legal encyclopedias.

Digests

Digests take the legally relevant points from a judicial opinion and organize those points according to topic. When a researcher looks up a particular legal topic, he or she will find a number of cases listed that pertain to that subject matter. The West Digest System is the most prominent national series of legal digests in use today.

Legal Encyclopedias

Legal encyclopedias are valuable tools for the legal researcher because they provide an overview of explanatory material on a number of legal topics. *Corpus Juris Secondum* (C.J.S.2d), *American Jurisprudence 2d* (Am.Jur.2d), and *West's Encyclopedia of American Law* are the best-known versions of legal encyclopedias.

Forms

There are a number of documents that you or your attorney will need to file in a divorce case. Most of these should be in a standard format. In fact, some local courts have preprinted blank forms available that you are required to use when filing pleadings. Other forms can be prepared by using the standard form, drafted according to state or local court rules, but with changes or additions as necessary for your particular case. An attorney who regularly practices in the area of family law should have a whole collection of divorce forms in his or her office computer that can be prepared simply by dropping in the names of the parties and other specifics from a case. Occasionally, you or your attorney will have to draft a document from scratch. A *formbook* is a compilation of blank forms pertaining to various topics, which you may use to create suitable pleadings for filing in your own case. Some formbooks are state-law specific, so that the blank forms are designed to meet the pleading requirements of your state. Other form-books are more general, which means you or your lawyer will need to know the particular technical requirements for pleadings in your county and state.

At **www.sphinxlegal.com/extras/quickiedivorce**, there are a number of blank forms relating to divorce practice. These forms are general, so you should research if and how they need to be altered in order to be used in your jurisdiction.

Changes in the Law

Remember that the law can change at any time. If the supreme court in your state reverses an appellate court case that you were planning to use in support of your own case, the appellate opinion will no longer be good precedent. Even though research materials in law libraries generally are kept current, there is a lag time between when a law changes and when libraries receive printed material with those changes. Moreover, information obtained from the Internet may not be accurate or current. For these reasons, you must be diligent in double-checking any supplementary materials to the statutes and cases you are citing to make sure that they remain good law.

In order to be sure your research is current, update all cases and statutes on which you are planning to rely. In the law library, supplementary materials usually can be found on the same shelf as the series of volumes you are using for your research. Often, but not always, the most recent update will be a softcover book or pamphlet. It also may appear as a *pocket part*, which is a paper pamphlet that actually fits into a built-in pocket in the back cover of certain legal books. The law librarian should be able to locate any relevant updates for you quickly.

To speed up this process, you might want to use an online service, such as Shepard's Citations Service, at **www.lexisnexis.com/shepards**. There are fees for the use of Shepard's online, so you may have to decide between saving time and saving money.

CHAPTER 4: The Divorce Case

A true quickie divorce is the exception rather than the rule. Given that, this chapter takes you briefly through the steps involved with obtaining a divorce, and wherever possible, suggests ways to shorten the time involved in completing each step. If a topic requires more in-depth discussion, it is taken up in a later chapter.

Preparation for the Case

The steps you must consider as a party to a divorce case may be different depending on whether you are the *petitioner* or the *respondent*. The petitioner is the person who initially files the lawsuit asking for a divorce; the respondent is the other spouse who must answer the lawsuit.

In some cases, the petitioner can be at an advantage because he or she can prepare and file the action without the the other person even knowing about it until he or she receives formal notice that the action has been filed. In such a case, the respondent may have to scramble to put together information that will be necessary to file a response to the lawsuit. It is important, however, to be as thorough as possible in collecting information, so that the attorney has a clear picture of what is at stake.

Whether you are the petitioner or the respondent, you will need to put together relevant information in order to prepare your case. If you do not have a certain document, try to recreate the information to the best of your ability. For example, if you cannot locate your tax returns for the last several years, you may be able to obtain copies of your recent W-2 forms from your employer, which you then may use to reconstruct the returns.

What follows is a checklist of the information that you should be prepared to bring to your attorney in order to prepare pleadings in support of your case. Some of the items in the list may not be pertinent to your case; however, it is better to have too much information for your lawyer than too little.

Information Checklist

Each spouse should try to gather as much of the following information as possible:

❑ personal information, including:
  ❑ full name
  ❑ birth date
  ❑ birth certificate
  ❑ marriage certificate
  ❑ Social Security number
  ❑ copy of driver's license
  ❑ highest education level attained
  ❑ occupation
  ❑ name and address of employer
  ❑ date and place of marriage
  ❑ names and birth dates of children
  ❑ length of residence in state
  ❑ information about prior marriages and children
  ❑ date of separation
  ❑ grounds for divorce
❑ paycheck stubs for the past 6–12 months for both spouses, if possible

❏ tax returns, including W-2s, 1099s, and all attachments for the last three years

❏ statements for all checking, savings, or other financial institution accounts for the last six months, including account numbers

❏ all life insurance policies owned by either spouse, including the insurance company, policy number, policyholder, annual premium, and amount of the benefit

❏ statement and/or plan description of any of the following in which either spouse has an interest:
  ❏ profit-sharing
  ❏ pension
  ❏ Keogh
  ❏ credit union accounts
  ❏ certificates of deposit
  ❏ brokerage accounts
  ❏ annuities
  ❏ retirement plans
  ❏ individual retirement accounts (IRAs)
  ❏ deferred compensation
  ❏ stock options

❏ health or dental insurance policies or other health plan to which either spouse belongs

❏ any other insurance policy held by either spouse, including but not limited to disability or homeowner's insurance

❏ documentation relating to any safe-deposit boxes held by either spouse

❏ stocks or bonds owned by either spouse, including purchase date and purchase price

❏ net worth or other financial statements created in the past 3–5 years for the purpose of obtaining a loan

❏ prenuptial or postnuptial agreement

❏ if applicable, information regarding prior marriage(s), including length of the marriage, children born of the marriage, and termination of the marriage

❏ wills or trusts prepared for or on behalf of either spouse

❏ wills or trusts in which either spouse is a beneficiary

❑ any inheritance or future interest in which either spouse has an interest

❑ birth certificate and Social Security cards for each child

❑ school records for each child

❑ college costs for children, including:

> ❑ tuition
>
> ❑ room and board
>
> ❑ books
>
> ❑ fees
>
> ❑ transportation

❑ any assets belonging to children

❑ work-related child care expenses for all children

❑ religious upbringing for children—past and future

❑ any written agreement relating to spousal or child support, custody, or marital property

❑ deed, address, tax number, and legal description of any real property owned by either spouse

❑ mortgage documents, tax assessments, or tax bills for real property owned by either spouse

❑ any real estate appraisal for real property for the last 3–5 years

❑ for any business interests owned by either spouse, partnership agreements or articles of incorporation, along with partnership or corporate tax returns for the last 3–5 years, along with all attachments and schedules

❑ for any business interests owned by either spouse, any accounts receivable ledgers or profit and loss statements for the past 3–5 years

❑ inventory of personal property belonging to either spouse separately or both spouses jointly, including approximate value and who owns each

❑ inventory of debts belonging to either spouse separately or both spouses jointly, including date debt was incurred, amount of current debt, and name and address of creditor for each debt

All of this information can help you and your attorney plan the strategy for your case. It also will make it easier to prepare the necessary pleadings and affidavits to proceed with the action.

Dissecting the Pleadings

Pleadings are documents prepared by the parties to a lawsuit or their attorneys, which are used to bring various matters to the attention of the judge in a court case. Pleadings in most states follow a similar basic form. At the top of the first page, note the *jurisdiction* of the court, which is the state, district, and/or county in which the court has authority to rule on cases. This is called the *heading*. Under this is usually found the *caption*, which includes the names of the parties and the case number that has been assigned by the court clerk. After that will typically be the *title*, which describes the matter that is being brought to the court's attention.

Then comes the *body* of the pleading, which sets out, paragraph by paragraph, what the party is asking for and why the party believes he or she should get that ruling. Each fact the party lists to support the petition should be a separate paragraph. After the body, there usually will be a *prayer for relief*, which is where the party makes a specific, detailed request for a ruling in his or her favor. Finally, at the end of most pleadings will come the signature of the party making the pleading. Sometimes the party him- or herself will sign the pleading, and other times the attorney may sign on behalf of the party. An example of a pleading, with the various parts labeled, appears on page 26. Other blank form pleadings can be found at **www.sphinxlegal.com/extras/quickiedivorce**.

IN THE CIRCUIT COURT OF THE FIRST JUDICIAL CIRCUIT
DAKOTA COUNTY, EAST DAKOTA

IN RE	)	
THE MARRIAGE OF:	)	
	)	
JANE JONES	)	
Petitioner,	)	Case No. 07D1234
and	)	
JOHN JONES	)	
Respondent.	)	

WIFE'S MOTION FOR HUSBAND TO PAY BILLS

NOW COMES Jane Jones, Petitioner in this matter, by and through her attorney, and hereby moves the Court for an order requiring the Respondent to pay the following bills, and in support thereof states as follows:

1. The following bills are outstanding and need to be paid:

Dr. Robert Smith, DDS (dentist)	$157.00
Dr. Victor Johnson, DVM (veterinarian)	$173.00
Stuffington Academy (tuition)	<u>$598.00</u>
Total:	$928.00

Copies of the above bills are attached hereto as Exhibit 'A'.

Petitioner does not have sufficient monies to pay these bills as the amount she is currently receiving from Respondent as spousal support is insufficient to cover these extra expenses.

Respondent is employed and is well able to pay these while Petitioner is currently unemployed but actively seeking employment and is unable at this time to pay same.

WHEREFORE, Petitioner respectfully requests this Honorable Court to enter an order requiring Respondent to pay the above immediately.

_____
Jane Jones
Petitioner

Depending on the pleading requirements for a particular state, some documents only need to be signed by the party, while others will need to be *verified*, which means the party must affirm that the allegations in the pleading are true when signing the document. Then, a notary public must certify the signature. Verified pleadings often are required when the party is making statements of fact. The court requires verification in such a case in order to subject the party to penalties for perjury, if the party makes statements in the pleading that are not true. A verification generally looks like this:

STATE OF EAST DAKOTA)
)

COUNTY OF DAKOTA   )

Jane Jones, being first duly sworn on oath, deposes and states that she has read the foregoing document, and the answers made herein are true, correct, and complete to the best of her knowledge and belief.

    Jane Jones
SIGNATURE

SUBSCRIBED and SWORN to before me this 4th day of October, 2007.

    Nancy Notary
NOTARY PUBLIC
My commission expires:
November 1, 2008

Petition and Initial Documents

The first pleading you will need to draft is the **Petition for Dissolution of Marriage**. (see sample form 1, p.230.) This is the document that, when filed with the clerk of the court in your county, starts the divorce case. It formally asks the court to end your marriage. In the petition, you will have to plead all of the facts required by your state's law in order to entitle you to the outcome you are seeking. At the very least in most states, you will have to set out when and where you were married, how long you have resided in the state, information about your children, and the facts that provide you with grounds for asking for a divorce. Residency requirements and grounds for divorce are discussed later.

A standard blank **Petition for Dissolution of Marriage** can be found at **www.sphinxlegal.com/extras/quickiedivorce**. This may be helpful in preparing a suitable pleading, although again, you should check the technical pleading requirements for your jurisdiction. If you have trouble determining how to fill out a petition, there is a sample **Petition for Dissolution of Marriage** in Appendix C that has been completed with fictitious information, just to give you an idea of how the document should appear. (see form 1, p.230.)

Many states require various other documents to be filed at the same time as the petition. Typically, if there are children involved, courts require an affidavit to be filed that meets the requirements of the *Uniform Child Custody Jurisdiction and Enforcement Act* (UCCJEA). The UCCJEA is a law in most states that makes it easier for one state to enforce a child custody order when one of the parents takes a child out of state when he or she is not supposed to. In a few states where the UCCJEA has not yet been enacted, its predecessor, the Uniform Child Custody Jurisdiction Act, governs, although the affidavit requirement is similar for both acts. Through the affidavit, the petitioner swears under oath that the state where the case is filed is the proper jurisdiction. A sample **UCCJEA Affidavit** can be found in Appendix C. (see form 7, p.247.)

Another document that courts routinely require to be filed with the petition is a *financial affidavit*. This is a sworn and notarized document that lists the parties' assets and liabilities, and helps the court make decisions about marital property and spousal support. A sample **Financial Affidavit** is included in Appendix C. (see form 6, p.243.)

When one spouse files an action in court for dissolution of marriage, the other spouse must receive notice of the proceeding and an opportunity to be heard in the matter. Therefore, in addition to the petition, it is necessary to prepare a document called a *summons*, which is a notice of the pending action. A sample **Summons** is included in Appendix C. (see form 3, p.238.) However, courts often will have their own forms for a summons that must be used.

Filing

When your documents have all been prepared, the next step is filing them with the proper court. You already should have determined which court has jurisdiction before you drafted your pleadings. *Jurisdiction* refers to which court is allowed to hear a particular case. Each state has its own requirements for the exercise of jurisdiction over family law matters. In general, at least one of the parties must have lived within the state for a certain amount of time right before the filing of the petition in order for the state's courts to have jurisdiction over the case. This is called a *residency* requirement.

In addition to jurisdiction, you should also think about *venue*, which is the location of the proper court in which to file a petition. In a state court action like a divorce, venue usually is appropriate in the trial court of the county in which one of the parties lives. In some states, it is the county in which the petitioner lives; in others, the petition must be filed in the county in which the respondent lives. In some states, either county is appropriate. Appendix B provides state-by-state information about what venue is proper.

To file a petition, response, or other pleading, bring the original document to the courthouse. It is a good idea to bring an extra copy as well, for your own records. Filed documents usually are given a date stamp by the clerk. Ask him or her to stamp your copy as well.

Usually there is a filing fee for certain documents filed with the court clerk. The fee is different in each county. Often the fee will include a charge for having the county sheriff serve copies of the summons and petition upon the other spouse. In some cases, an indigent petitioner can ask the court to waive filing fees, if he or she can show in an affidavit why he or she cannot afford them.

Service

For a court to have jurisdiction over a respondent in a divorce (or any other) action, the respondent must have received proper notice of the case. To give notice, the petitioner must *serve* the respondent with a copy of the lawsuit, in a manner set forth by state law.

Usually, you cannot serve notice to someone else yourself. Instead, service of the summons and petition, also called *service of process*, must be made either by the sheriff of the county in which the respondent resides or by a special private process server who is registered in the state. The summons and petition must be given either directly to the respondent or to someone who lives in the respondent's household who is above a certain age, typically 13.

Some states also allow service by publication in a newspaper. Usually this is allowed only after physical service of process has been unsuccessful. When that happens, the petitioner files an affidavit stating that he or she made a *good faith* effort to locate the other party, has been unable to do so, and does not know where the other party is. In general, states that allow service by publication also only allow the court to order the dissolution of the marriage; orders for maintenance, child support, and child custody usually may not be made in a case in which service is by publication.

Once the sheriff or process server has served the respondent, he or she completes an *affidavit of service*, stating under oath that the respondent was served with the summons and petition. This is proof that the respondent has notice of the pending action. Anyone who receives such notice and does not respond to the petition does so at the risk of having a judgment entered without being allowed to present his or her case.

Response

Once a respondent is served with the summons and petition, he or she generally has a certain amount of time to file a response—usually twenty or thirty days, depending on the jurisdiction. If the respondent is unable to file a response within the time allowed, the respondent must file a request for additional time. The request itself must be filed within the time period for a response. If the respondent fails to file any response or request for more time in which to answer, he or she may be found in *default* by the court. This means that he or she may not be allowed to file pleadings in the case at all, and the petitioner may be automatically awarded whatever he or she asked for in the petition. For that reason, it is extremely important that if you are served with a petition for dissolution, you find a lawyer as soon as possible so that your attorney meets the filing deadline and avoids default.

If there is some sort of technical problem with the petition or the manner in which it was served, the respondent might attempt to answer with a *motion to strike* or a *motion to dismiss* the petition, which, if granted, would end the matter on a technicality. However, the court usually will give the petitioner the opportunity to correct the defect, so this tactic may serve only to delay the proceedings.

If there is no reason to file a motion to dismiss, the respondent should file a document answering each specific allegation of the petition, either with an admission, a denial, or a statement that the respondent has insufficient knowledge of the facts of the allegation to admit or deny. If you are a respondent, you will have to decide whether you agree or disagree with the allegations of the petition and what it asks for. If you want to contest the division of marital property that the petitioner is seeking or if you are not satisfied with the custody arrangement that is requested, you should set out in your response your reasons for disagreement. If your spouse is asking for sole or primary custody against your wishes, you should consider making your own request for custody in your response. A sample **Response to Petition for Dissolution** is included in Appendix C. (see form 5, p.240.)

Discovery

The process of *discovery* is the means by which a party to a dissolution action can get information when the other party will not provide it voluntarily. State law rules allow certain ways that each side can demand information and evidence from the other. The rules also provide penalties for refusal to comply with these requests. Various methods of discovery are discussed in the following sections.

Interrogatories

Interrogatories are written questions submitted to the other party to be answered under oath. Some states provide limits to the number of interrogatories that may be asked without further permission of the court. This limit generally includes subparts of questions. Otherwise, it is necessary to request that the court allow you to send out additional interrogatories. Such a request usually is granted only in limited circumstances where good cause is shown.

Upon receipt of the interrogatories, the recipient has a certain amount of time, usually around twenty-eight days, in which to respond with either a sworn answer or an objection to each interrogatory. The interrogatories must be relevant to the proceeding at hand, or the recipient's attorney probably will object to the interrogatory, and will advise the recipient not to answer the particular question. If additional information pertaining to an interrogatory becomes known to the recipient party after the original response is submitted, the recipient has a duty to add to the original response. The answers given to the interrogatories may be used as evidence at trial.

It might help to think of the various types of discovery as building blocks that are used to construct your case. It is probably smart to direct interrogatories to the other party as a first step of discovery. That way, you can collect preliminary information, which hopefully will help you determine what other data needs to be obtained, such as which documents need to be subpoenaed and what facts should be admitted by the other party.

Request to Admit Facts

If you believe there are facts that are not being disputed by the other party, you can submit a *request to admit facts* to the other party. This is a series of written assertions of fact, to which the other party must respond under oath. The response will be in the form of an admission, a denial, or a statement that the other party is unable to admit or deny and the reason why. Having admissions of the other party to a set of facts will save time and effort at trial, by narrowing the scope of issues that are in dispute.

Request to Produce and Subpoena for Documents

If you find from the other party's responses to your interrogatories and request to admit facts that there are documents in existence that would be helpful to your case, the next step is to compel production of those documents. If the documents are in the hands of your spouse, you should serve him or her with a Request for Production. A sample **Request for Production** can be found in Appendix C. (see form 9, p. 258.) If the documents are in the possession of a third party, such as a bank or the other party's employer, you will need to serve the third party with a subpoena for documents. The documents you are seeking must be listed with some particularity, and must be relevant to the issues in your case. Otherwise, the other party may object to the subpoena or request to produce as being an overly broad *fishing expedition* for documents. The respondent will have a certain period of time within which to respond to the request.

If you are served with a request to produce documents, you may respond either by forwarding copies of the documents asked for, or if there is an extremely large amount of documents, you may provide a reasonable time and place for the other side to examine documents that they wish to discover. If you have a specific objection to producing a certain document—for example, if it is subject to a legal privilege and does not have to be disclosed (communications between you and your attorney fall under this category), you may respond to the request by stating in writing that you object to the request and why you object. However, no matter what your response, it must be given within the time period allowed for answering. If you have a good reason for not being able to respond in a timely manner, you should ask the other side for more time. If the other side is not agreeable, you will have to make a formal motion to the court for an extended period in which to respond.

Subpoenas to Compel Appearance

The actual parties to a divorce proceeding are required to appear for a hearing, and if they do not, they risk having the court rule in favor of the other party by default. What if there is a third-party witness that you wish to depose or call at trial? Third parties must be summoned by means of a *subpoena*, which can be served by certified or registered mail and must include a witness fee and mileage costs as provided by statute.

Depositions

In a *deposition*, a witness, called the *deponent*, is placed under oath and asked a series of questions by the attorney for one of the parties. The testimony is recorded by a court reporter, and can be used as evidence at trial. The witness can be one of the litigants or a third party. Parties themselves are called to a deposition by means of a *notice to appear*, delivered to the party's attorney. Third parties are summoned by means of a subpoena. If the person you want to depose is expected to give testimony favorable to your case, consult with him or her to schedule the deposition, at his or her convenience if possible. You do not want to alienate the witness by having a subpoena showing up unexpectedly. Even though a deposition is a routine procedure, it may be intimidating to someone who is unfamiliar with the course of a legal proceeding.

As with a request for production, the questions asked of the witness must be relevant to the proceeding giving rise to the deposition, or the attorney for the other party is likely to object. If that happens, any objectionable question will have to be presented to the court for a determination as to whether it is proper.

When preparing interrogatories, your attorney should include a request that the other party list all witnesses to be called at trial, and that he or she disclose the subject of each witness's testimony. You then can decide which of the potential witnesses should be deposed. Although the cost of taking depositions can mount quickly after you have paid the court reporter and transcription costs, it is better that you depose as many of the other side's listed witnesses as possible to avoid unpleasant surprises at trial. In addition, deposing witnesses will get their sworn testimony on the record so that if a witness attempts to change his or her story at trial, your attorney will be able to use the prior deposition testimony to discredit the witness.

Chances are that you also will be called to give a deposition by the other side. Your attorney should be present during the deposition and should prepare you for giving testimony beforehand. A good lawyer will foresee questions that are likely to be asked. At the time of the deposition, he or she should object to any question asked that is improper.

Although depositions can be intimidating for a nonlawyer, testifying at one is different from testifying in court. Whatever you say will be transcribed by a court reporter, and if your testimony comes up again at a later time during the litigation, a third party will simply read it out loud. So, if you stammer or your hands shake because you are nervous, or if you take a long time to answer questions, it will not show up in the written transcript.

Request for Examination

In a case where you believe that the mental or physical condition of either the other spouse or one of your minor children is at issue, you can request that the court order a mental or physical evaluation of that person. Even if you do not request such an examination, the court has the power to require such an examination on its own. A psychiatric evaluation of a minor child may be useful if you have reason to believe that your spouse is doing psychological harm to the child, or if you think that your spouse has psychiatric or psychological issues affecting his or her ability to adequately parent your child.

◆◆◆

From the perspective of a person wanting to end a marriage as quickly as possible, the discovery process may seem to be a large obstacle. It may be tempting to send off a series of written discovery requests at the same time depositions are scheduled, in order to save time. It is better, however, to conduct discovery in a particular order. To use discovery to the fullest, your attorney should wait until he or she receives answers to interrogatories before scheduling the other party for a deposition. That way, the lawyer can use the other party's written answers to help him or her decide what questions to ask when deposing the other party. If a particular written answer is nonresponsive, your attorney can seek clarification at the deposition. Depositions serve the additional purpose of allowing you to see how a potential witness conducts him- or herself under examination by attorneys. This will help you evaluate which of the other party's witnesses will be most credible, and possibly most damaging to your case.

Custody Evaluation

When a divorce case involves minor children of the parties, and there has been no agreement regarding custody or visitation rights, courts usually will order a *custody evaluation*, which is a series of interviews and psychological screenings of parents, children, and any other individual who may be able to provide insight into the best interests of the children.

In a psychiatric evaluation for custody purposes, the subject is likely to be given several tests, which serve to measure the subject's personality traits and responses to various real-life situations. The tests are designed to correct for the possibility that some subjects may give answers they consider to be the "right" answer, even if the answer given is not honest. Some of these tests also are used to uncover indicators of the potential for mental illness.

The evaluator also will interview the subject, and may interview others whom the evaluator believes can provide relevant information. Sometimes the evaluator will ask the subject to provide the names of people who know and are willing to answer questions about him or her. The evaluator might then speak to these people, or might provide them with a written questionnaire for them to complete and return to the evaluator. The evaluator will take the information provided by all concerned, along with the test results and his or her own opinions, and will make a report of his or her findings, which may include a recommendation as to custody. This recommendation of the custody evaluator is a crucial piece of evidence, one to which a court may give a great deal of weight.

Pretrial Conference

The purpose of a pretrial hearing or conference is to focus the issues that the judge will be asked to rule upon at trial, and to clear up any lingering matters that need to be settled before trial, such as any outstanding discovery requests or objections to evidence or witnesses that the other party will seek to produce at trial. Often, the judge will ask the attorneys to state their clients' positions, in the hope that the judge can recommend a resolution upon which the parties can agree and thus avoid going to trial. If there is no settlement at the pretrial hearing, the judge will set a trial date.

Trial

The *trial* is the formal presentation of evidence and legal arguments in support of each party's case. The admissibility of evidence presented in court is subject to formal requirements under state law. An in-depth discussion of the rules of evidence is beyond the scope of this book. In general, any physical evidence, photographs, documents, or witness testimony that you want the court to consider must be credible and relevant to the issues at stake in your case. In addition, any documents presented must be authentic.

The procedure at trial generally follows a certain pattern. First, the petitioner's attorney gives an opening statement, in which he or she provides an overview of the petitioner's position and the evidence that will be presented at trial. Then, the respondent's attorney makes his or her own opening statement. After this, physical evidence and witness testimony are presented. Each of the petitioner's witnesses will be *examined*—asked— questions by the petitioner's attorney. After one witness is examined directly, the other party then will have the opportunity to *cross-examine* the witness regarding the answers the witness gave on direct examination.

If one side believes the court should disregard a certain piece of evidence or a witness statement, that attorney will *object* to the admission of the evidence. The court will rule on each objection as it is made, either by sustaining the objection (agreeing with the objection and refusing to allow the evidence) or overruling the objection (disagreeing with the objection and allowing the evidence). It is necessary to object to any problematic evidence in order to be able to raise the issue on appeal.

Expert Testimony

The testimony of *experts* can be crucial to a dissolution action. Financial experts may be used to support a party's argument that more or less maintenance should be paid, for example. Health care professionals and physicians, in particular, may be invaluable in assisting the court in determining the best interest of the child in a custody dispute. Experts may be appointed by the court, or they may be called by the parties to testify in support of a party's particular position. In the latter case, the expert witness, along with the subject of his or her expected testimony, must be disclosed to the other party prior to trial. In any case, if you plan to introduce expert opinion testimony, whether from a professional that you have retained or from an expert who has evaluated the case pursuant to a court order, be sure that you know what that expert will say *before* you list him or her as a witness. Again, it is best to avoid surprises.

Your Own Testimony

As a witness in the case, you also need to be prepared by your attorney to testify. For many people, this case will be the first time they have ever found themselves on a witness stand. It can be an intimidating experience. The most important thing to remember is to tell the truth. If you have been honest with your attorney so far, hopefully he or she can mitigate the effect of negative testimony. At the same time, you should take care not to volunteer more information than you are asked for, whether it is your attorney or the other party's who is doing the asking. Some people, because they are nervous on the witness stand, keep talking even after they have responded to the attorney's question. Make your answer short and sweet, and then sit silently until the next question is asked. If you do not know the answer to a question, simply state that you do not know. If the other party's attorney asks you an inappropriate question on cross-examination, it is your attorney's job to object to the question. If the other attorney asks you a question that is confusing to you, or that assumes an answer, state that you do not under-stand or are not able to answer the question as it has been posed. If the other attorney asks you a question that requires you to give an answer that has a negative effect on your case, or that impeaches your credibility, your attorney will have a chance to rehabilitate your testimony on redirect examination.

Above all, try not to let your nerves get to you. Take a deep, calming breath, if necessary, before answering. Try to remain fairly still on the stand, because leg-bouncing, finger-tapping, and other nervous behaviors can be distracting to the judge as he or she tries to listen to your testimony.

Conduct and Appearance in Court

Even if you have an attorney representing you, your own appearance and manners may have an impact on the judge's decision in your case. Therefore, you should know what is expected of those appearing in court.

First of all, you should be well groomed. It is not necessary for you to have an expensive suit or designer clothes, but you should be clean and your outfit should be in good repair. Men with long hair, beards, and so on, should not be unkempt. If you show that you care how you look, it sends a message to the judge that you should be taken seriously.

Second, you should not be late to court. If your case is called and you are not present, your attorney will have to ask that the case be held until the judge has finished the rest of his or her business. This will inconvenience the court, and also may tell the judge that this proceeding is not of the utmost importance to you.

Finally, you should use proper manners before the judge, even if you are in the spectator area waiting for your case to be called. Do not speak loudly or rudely, do not use bad language, and do not make any threatening remarks or gestures. There are bailiffs present who will remove you from the courtroom.

Beyond that, use common manners. Do not chew gum or bring food or drinks to court. Do not pull out a newspaper. Turn off your pager and cell phone. Many judges instruct their bailiffs to forbid litigants from bringing these items into the courtroom at all. When speaking to the judge, address him or her as "Your Honor," "Sir," or "Ma'am."

Regardless of the outcome of your court date, tell the judge "thank you" when the proceedings are finished, and save any outbursts for some time after you have left the courtroom. Particularly in contentious cases, where you may find yourself before this judge on a number of occasions, it is important to give the impression that you are serious about your case and that you respect the court's authority in the matter.

After all the evidence has been submitted, the parties each may make a closing argument. This is a summary of what has already been presented to the court, along with citations to the applicable law, and argument as to why the court should rule in favor of that particular party. The petitioner's side goes first. This is your last chance to argue your case, so it is best to be sure the argument is well organized, to the point, and supported by the evidence that has been presented.

Decree of Dissolution

After all of the evidence has been presented and the arguments made, the judge will render a decision in the form of a *decree of dissolution*, or *divorce decree*. It should cover all of the issues that were raised in the pleadings and at trial, including property distribution and child custody. If the parties have agreed to a property settlement or custody arrangement outside of court, whether before or after the court has heard evidence, the agreement must be submitted to the judge for his or her approval.

Under certain circumstances, a divorce decree may be modified or terminated after it has been entered. Also, all states have procedures by which a divorce decree may be enforced if one of the parties does not abide by the order's terms. (see Chapter 13.)

Appeal

If the parties each decide that they can live with the dissolution decree entered by the court, the litigation ends. If, on the other hand, the outcome is unacceptable to one or both of the parties, the next step is to take the matter to a higher court through an *appeal*. The party wishing to file an appeal is called the *appellant*, and the one responding to the appeal is the *appellee*. Sometimes, both sides file appeals; in that case, the parties are *cross-appellants*. No new evidence is heard by the appellate court; only the transcribed record of the trial court proceedings, pleadings filed by the parties, and in some cases, oral argument presented by the attorneys are considered on appeal.

As with your decision to proceed with the divorce, you should carefully examine your motives if you are considering filing an appeal of a divorce decree. Appellate work is quite involved and may be expensive. It is more likely than not that the appellate court will refuse to overrule the trial court. Emotions run high in divorce matters, and sometimes the desire to achieve total victory over the other party can cloud an honest assessment of the merits of your position. Consider whether you want to take the chance of losing whatever you were granted by the trial court because there is no guarantee that the end result will be different even if you manage to have the trial court overruled. The case could be returned to the trial court for a new hearing, and the results of that hearing could be less favorable than what you received the first time around.

In order to challenge a final order by the trial court, the appellant must have grounds for the appeal. The most common grounds are either that the trial court made a mistake in applying the law or that the decision of the trial court was *against the manifest weight of the evidence*; that is, no reasonable judge who considered the evidence in this particular case could have come to the conclusion reached by the trial court. It is very difficult to succeed on appeal using the manifest weight argument. The trial court judge is the one who heard the testimony and reviewed the other evidence first-hand, and without a mistake in the application of the law, appellate courts are very hesitant to reverse a case on the basis that the trial judge incorrectly evaluated the facts before him or her.

Appellate rules in most states are extremely particular with regard to filing deadlines and pleading requirements. Some state appellate courts go so far as to require a certain size type when preparing appellate briefs. If you feel an appeal is in order, it is not the time to go it *pro se*. While trial courts sometimes are lenient with litigants, often giving parties a second or third chance to correct pleadings and file documents late, the appellate courts are not so forgiving.

CHAPTER 5:
Establishing Grounds for Divorce

A divorce petition must state grounds for dissolution. *Grounds* are the legal reason why a court should grant the request to end the marriage. Every state has its own set of grounds that you can use; certain grounds may be available in one state but unavailable in the next state over. Appendix B provides state-by-state information as to which grounds can be pleaded in each jurisdiction.

In relation to grounds, there are two types of divorce: traditional and no-fault. There are advantages and disadvantages to both. This chapter also discusses *covenant marriages*, which a few state legislatures have created in response to the popularity of *no-fault divorce*.

No-Fault Divorce

The trend toward no-fault divorce has made the pleading of traditional grounds unpopular. *No-fault divorce* means that the marriage has ended because of *irreconcilable differences*. This has become popular over the past few decades because the spouse filing for divorce does not need to provide proof of any of the traditional grounds for divorce, which can be difficult. It is enough to plead that the marriage is irretrievably broken, without blame becoming an issue. In some states, no-fault is the only option; traditional grounds have been eliminated in those states.

The main disadvantage to pursuing the no-fault divorce is that states generally require proof of a separation period before allowing the divorce to proceed. Depending on your state, the waiting period may be as much as two years. This requirement slows down the individual seeking a quick end to his or her marriage. However, keep in mind that many states do allow the parties to shorten or even waive the separation period if both sides agree.

Traditional Grounds

If you are unable or unwilling to go the route of a no-fault divorce, as a petitioner you will have to plead and prove one of the traditional grounds for divorce that is allowed in your state.

One advantage of pleading a traditional ground is that you can usually avoid being required to have a period of separation. For this reason, *traditional grounds* may be useful for those seeking a quick divorce, especially if the responding spouse does not contest the allegations. Also in some states, the fault of one party can be considered by the judge in making a division of marital property or award of child custody or maintenance.

On the other hand, the downside is that you have to produce evidence of whatever ground you are pleading, especially if the grounds are contested. For example, if you use your spouse's adultery as a ground for divorce and he or she denies it, you will have to prove the allegation in court.

All of the following are traditional grounds in at least one state; check the state-specific information in Appendix B to see which ones are available in your jurisdiction.

Mental Cruelty

Mental cruelty by one spouse toward the other is a traditional ground for divorce in a number of states. Although the legal definition is not necessarily the same in all jurisdictions, most agree that you need more than just one act of cruelty to establish the ground. There has to be a pattern of behavior, over a certain amount of time, by one spouse that endangers the mental health of the other spouse. Inconsiderate or annoying behavior is not enough. The conduct also must be intentional. Finally, there has to be an actual negative effect on the spouse enduring the cruelty, or at least a connection between the abusive spouse's actions and the breakdown of the marriage.

Adultery

Adultery is sexual relations between one spouse and another person who is not the other spouse. To use this ground, the petitioner does not have to prove the exact date or location of the adultery. However, merely a suspicion of infidelity is not enough. Generally, the petitioner must show that his or her spouse has had both the opportunity to commit adultery as well as the inclination to do so. For example, if you can prove that your spouse spent the night in a hotel with a person of the opposite sex, that should be enough to prove adultery.

Keep in mind, though, that if the wronged spouse has sexual relations with the adulterous spouse, in spite of knowing about the infidelity, then the grounds will be voided. This is because the law treats the resumption of marital relations as forgiveness of the adultery.

Impotence

Impotence is the inability of the husband to physically sustain sexual relations. It is not a ground for divorce in all states. In some states, it is grounds for annulment as well as for divorce. In several states, the impotence must have existed at the time of the marriage and continued through the time of the divorce. In others, current impotence is all that the petitioner must show.

Conviction of Crime

Typically, the ground for *conviction of a crime* requires a felony conviction of the respondent spouse. However, in some states, a misdemeanor conviction will be sufficient. Often, the state statute will require that the convicted spouse has been sentenced to a prison term of a certain length and has been incarcerated for a certain amount of that sentence, before the ground for divorce will take effect. For example, in Alabama, the convicted spouse must be imprisoned for at least two years of a seven-year sentence. In Virginia, on the other hand, all that is required is that the respondent spouse be convicted of a felony and sentenced, that he or she serves time for the conviction, and that the spouses have not resumed cohabitation after the imprisonment.

Insanity

In most states allowing *insanity* of a spouse to be grounds for divorce, the law requires some period of confinement, around two or three years, in a mental health institution before the petition is filed. Some states require a showing that the insanity is incurable. Also, some jurisdictions require a mental examination of the respondent spouse by a qualified physician before the court can grant a divorce. For annulment, most states require that the insanity existed at the time the parties entered the marriage.

Nonsupport

In general, *nonsupport* refers to one spouse's failure to provide for the other spouse and their family, even though he or she has the ability to do so. This ground requires that the refusal to support the spouse is deliberate. Therefore, the ground is not available to someone whose husband or wife simply is unable to provide support due to illness, injury, and so on. Not many states consider nonsupport to be an adequate ground for divorce.

Habitual Drunkenness or Drug Use

Different states allowing *habitual alcohol or drug use* as a ground for divorce have a variety of provisions defining what the petitioner must prove. In most states, the drug or alcohol use must have become a habit *after* the marriage. This is because the law assumes that if the habit existed before the marriage, the petitioning spouse must have known of and permitted the habit, and cannot come back later and say that the substance abuse was the cause for the breakup of the marriage. Some states require proof that the habit has existed for a certain period of time before the divorce action commenced—Illinois, for example, requires that habitual drunkenness has gone on for two years.

Some states even give guidance as to the level that the habit must reach in order for the ground to be available. The Illinois statute refers to the requirement that habitual drug use "becomes a controlling or a dominant purpose of [the respondent's] life." Habitual, however, does not mean that the responding spouse is constantly intoxicated. It simply means that the petitioner has to show a habit of regular and excessive alcohol or drug use by the respondent.

Desertion

In states where *desertion*—or *abandonment*, as it is known in some jurisdictions—is considered grounds for divorce, the usual requirements are that the desertion is deliberate and malicious, and that it continue for a minimum period of time. In some states, the court may find desertion after one year; in other states, it may be as many as seven years.

The act of desertion itself can mean different things in different states. In some jurisdictions, the abandoning spouse must physically pack up and leave, and then stay away for the necessary time period. This is known as *actual desertion*. The petitioning spouse also must show that the other spouse does not intend to return.

Typically, however, states also recognize what is called *constructive desertion*, which is when the abandoning spouse does not leave the home, but checks out of the marriage all the same. With constructive desertion, it is enough that the spouse intentionally refuses to participate in the marriage, such as by refusing to communicate with the petitioning spouse, refusing to engage in sexual relations with the petitioning spouse, or behaving in such a way as to threaten the health or well-being of the petitioning spouse.

However, desertion does not apply if the petitioning spouse is the one who drove the respondent away. This protects the spouse who leaves for his or her own well-being from being named as the at-fault party by the other spouse, when the other spouse is actually the one that caused the breakup of the marriage.

Bigamy

Bigamy simply means that the respondent spouse has another living spouse at the time of the marriage. In such a case, the later marriage is actually invalid and is viewed as never happening in the first place. For that reason, bigamy is also grounds for annulment, which is discussed in Chapter 1. Moreover, bigamy is a crime. It is a felony in some states, and a misdemeanor in others, but it is not prosecuted very often unless the perpetrator was making the bigamous marriages in order to rob his or her victims.

Homosexuality

Some jurisdictions recognize homosexuality as a separate ground for divorce, while others treat homosexual behavior as a subcategory of another ground, such as adultery, mental cruelty, or desertion. Under the laws of several states, homosexuality is not a cause for divorce at all, in which case a spouse seeking to end the marriage would have to pursue the no-fault option.

Sexually Transmitted Disease

Infection with a *sexually transmitted disease* of one spouse by the other spouse is grounds for divorce in only one state—Illinois—at present. However, in some jurisdictions, failure by one spouse to tell the other spouse at the time the marriage is entered into that he or she is infected with a communicable disease is considered a fraud that may be grounds for annulment.

Pregnancy by Another Man at Time of Marriage

A number of states will allow divorce based upon the fact that, at the time of the marriage, the wife is pregnant by a man other than her husband. However, these states generally require that, when the marriage is entered into, the husband is unaware that someone else is the father of the child. As with the case of sexually transmitted diseases, this would be considered a fraud, giving rise to grounds for annulment as well as divorce.

Marriage Obtained by Fraud, Force, or Duress

Most states are not in agreement regarding their treatment of marriages that one spouse secures by defrauding, forcing, or pressuring the other spouse to consent to the marriage. Some states consider such a situation to be a ground for divorce. Other states also treat these situations as grounds for annulment as well. Some states allow fraud, force, and duress to be grounds only for annulment, not for divorce. Still others do not allow these marriages to be terminated at all based on these circumstances.

As with adultery, if the petitioning spouse continues to live with the respondent spouse after becoming aware of the fraud or after the force or duress has ended, then the grounds will no longer be valid. The court will treat the petitioner as though he or she has forgiven the other spouse.

Consanguinity or Affinity

Consanguinity refers to closeness of a blood relationship between two people; for example, brother and sister. *Affinity* pertains to closeness of a relationship by marriage, such as a mother-in-law and son-in-law. For a marriage to be legal in a particular state, it must be between two people who are not within prohibited degrees of consanguinity or affinity.

Different states allow for different degrees of closeness between the marrying parties. In most states, second cousins can marry, but first cousins are too close in consanguinity. There are a handful of states, however, in which even first cousins are allowed to get married. Several states also specifically prohibit marriage between those within the prohibited degrees of affinity, generally those having an in-law relationship with each other.

Consanguinity and affinity may also be, or may alternatively be, grounds for annulment in several states. Most statutes addressing the issue include relatives of half-blood, "step" relatives, and relatives by adoption along with whole-blood relatives.

Deviant Sexual Conduct

A few jurisdictions allow divorce based on *deviant sexual conduct*, or *crimes against nature*, as it sometimes is referred to. This categorization may cover a variety of acts, but typically refers to sodomy and similar behavior. It is necessary that the other spouse does not agree with or condone the behavior. The petitioning spouse will lose the ability to plead this fault-based ground for divorce if he or she continues to cohabit with the responding spouse after becoming aware of the deviant sexual conduct.

Abuse of Spouse or Child of the Parties

The grounds of *abuse* appear in a number of states under various titles: *violence, cruel physical treatment, abusive treatment*. Some statutes base the grounds on abuse of the spouse, while others refer to abuse of the child, or both. These grounds are different from mental cruelty in that here it is the *physical* abuse that causes the breakup of the marriage.

Fault-based divorce may actually take less time than no-fault divorce. If you cannot convince your spouse to agree to waive the separation period that is required by many states' no-fault divorce statutes, the no-fault option could take an extra two years or more. Keep in mind, however, that many of the previously mentioned fault grounds will require *corroborating* evidence. That is, there must be actual evidence to support the claim on which you are relying to give you grounds for divorce—your own testimony will not be enough. Obtaining that evidence may be time-consuming; you might need to hire a private investigator to substantiate an adultery allegation, for example. This is yet another example of how cooperation between the parties is usually the best way to achieve a desirable result in a timely manner.

Covenant Marriage

Many people believe that no-fault divorce is the cause of increased divorce rates in recent years, by making it easier to end one's marriage. In response, a handful of states—only Arizona, Arkansas, and Louisiana at the time of publication—have enacted what are known as *covenant marriage* laws. Covenant marriages generally require a couple to have premarital counseling. In addition, the couple must agree to waive their right to pursue a no-fault divorce. Only adultery, abuse, felony conviction with imprisonment, or a lengthy separation will open the door for a party to terminate a covenant marriage.

Some have criticized the idea of covenant marriage, saying it is religion interfering with what should be a strictly governmental area of regulation. Regardless of the criticism, however, covenant marriage does not seem to have caught on. Statistically, very few couples seeking marriage licenses in the covenant marriage states have selected this option.

CHAPTER 6:
Residency Requirements

For purposes of divorce law, *residence* refers to the main home state of a party to the divorce proceeding. While you may have two or more residences in actuality, when you file a divorce petition, you will have to show that you are filing in the state that has appropriate jurisdiction over the case. Usually, the state in which either the husband or the wife is physically present and in which he or she is planning on staying will be the right place to file.

In some jurisdictions, though, other factors might let the court exercise its authority over divorce cases. Some states will allow jurisdiction if the event that caused the marriage to break up occurred in that state. Others do not have a residency requirement for the petitioner if the marriage occurred in that state. There are even a few jurisdictions that simply have no required time period of residency at all, so long as the petitioner did not move to the state for the sole purpose of obtaining a divorce.

It is not necessary that you work in the state in which you live. Moreover, you generally are not required to remain a resident of the state throughout the entire divorce proceeding. However, if children are involved, you could be restricted from moving out of state with them.

Establishing and Proving Residency

Because you need to show physical presence and intent to remain in a state, corroborating evidence showing these might be needed if you have to prove residency. One of the clearest indications of residency is proof of where you live. A deed to your home; a lease; or utility, telephone, or cable bills coming to your home address are useful to show residency. Voter's registration documentation also is helpful, as are a driver's license and a library card.

Changing Residency

The petitioner's state of residence may be an important consideration if time is of the essence in obtaining a divorce. If the law would be more favorable to you if you lived one state over, it might be worth your while to think about relocating. Keep in mind, however, that some states specifically prohibit residency that is undertaken only for the purpose of getting a divorce.

Appendix B provides state-by-state information on the topics of residency requirements and grounds for divorce, among others. You can compare the law of your home state with that of nearby states, to determine whether one statute will be more favorable to you. If it is advantageous to file in another state, and your situation allows you to relocate—that is, you can move your job and your children, if necessary—you could consider actually changing your state of residency in order to move your divorce along more quickly.

Analyze residency requirements carefully if you are thinking of relocation, especially if you are nearer to achieving residency where you are. If you have lived in a jurisdiction long enough to establish residency for purposes of divorce, and you then move to another state, the time period starts over again if you decide to return to the first state to live.

EXAMPLE:

Assume you and your spouse were both raised in Rhode Island and lived there your entire lives. Then you both move to Massachusetts. Three months after moving there, you decide you wish to file for divorce because of marital problems you both already had before the move, and you return home to Rhode Island.

Although you had established residency in Rhode Island and could have filed for divorce there before you moved out of state, you lost that residency by relocating to Massachusetts, where the residency requirement is one year (unless the grounds for the divorce occurred there, in which case there is no residency requirement). You have three months under your belt in Massachusetts, whereas if you return to Rhode Island, the clock begins ticking again and you will have to wait the statutory twelve months required to establish residency in Rhode Island once again.

If your only interest is in obtaining a divorce as quickly as possible, then you may wish to remain in Massachusetts, in order to establish residency in only nine more months. There may be other, more compelling reasons to return to Rhode Island, however. For one, the law may be more favorable to your case in that state. Another consideration is that you may have family, friends, and an established life and system of moral support in Rhode Island. Just be aware of the possibility that the quickest way to a divorce may not necessarily be the best way for you to proceed.

Residency Requirements Chart

The following chart shows the ten states with the longest residency requirements, and the adjacent states to each that have the shortest requirements.

State	Residency Requirement	Nearby State(s) with Lowest Requirement
Connecticut	1 year	No adjacent state has shorter requirement (except Massachusetts, which has none if the grounds for divorce occurred there)
Iowa	1 year	Illinois (90 days); South Dakota (none)
Maryland	1 year	DC, Virginia (6 months each)
Nebraska	1 year	South Dakota (none), Kansas (60 days)
New Hampshire	1 year	Vermont, Maine (6 months each)
New Jersey	1 year	Pennsylvania, Delaware (6 months each)
New York	1 year	Vermont, Ohio, Pennsylvania (6 months each)
Rhode Island	1 year	No adjacent state has shorter requirement (except Massachusetts, which has none if the grounds for divorce occurred there)
Washington	1 year	Idaho (6 weeks)
West Virginia	1 year	Ohio, Pennsylvania, Virginia, Kentucky (6 months each)

CHAPTER 7:
Foreign Divorce

The term *foreign divorce* can refer to a divorce granted in either another state or another country. You need to know whether or not a divorce obtained in a jurisdiction that is not your state of residency will be treated as valid by your home state.

Divorce from Another State

The Full Faith and Credit Clause of the U.S. Constitution requires that each state recognize the judicial orders of every other state as if they were coming from its own courts. There are only a few limitations to this doctrine. When the judicial order of another state goes against the public policy of the state being asked to recognize the order, the state can refuse to uphold the order. When it comes to orders relating to marriage, usually the only orders another state will not honor are those allowing polygamy, incest, or same-sex marriage. Otherwise, if your divorce is valid in the state from which you obtained the order, it is valid in any other state.

Divorce from a Foreign Country

When most people hear the phrase *quickie divorce*, they probably think of a short jaunt to the Caribbean, where one spouse can plunk down some money, fill out some paperwork, and be divorced within a few days.

Websites abound with offers of fast divorces from the Dominican Republic, Haiti, and even by mail order. They make it sound like a fresh start is only a hop, skip, and jump away.

Alas, it is not that simple. In fact, mail-order divorces from other countries are invalid in the United States, period. The U.S. Constitution is not applicable to divorce rulings coming from other countries. While the federal government has a reason to require states to honor each other's judicial processes, there is no such incentive when it comes to the legal systems of other governments. As a result, each state is left to determine whether a divorce decree of another country will be recognized in that state.

Comity

Often, states will uphold foreign countries' judicial orders anyway because of a principle known as *comity*. This is a courtesy extended by the court of one country toward a court from another country. The court that is asked to honor a foreign court order recognizes and defers to the authority of the court originally making the ruling.

In most cases, for a state to recognize a foreign order, one of the parties has to be physically present in the foreign country during the divorce without any immediate intent to leave the foreign country.

Ex Parte and Bilateral Proceedings

In some states, whether or not a state court will recognize an order of another country's court depends on whether the respondent ever received proper notice of the divorce in order to have a fair chance to participate in the divorce proceedings. *Proper notice* means that the responding party must be served with process, as discussed in Chapter 4.

When one spouse travels to another country for a divorce without the other spouse present, the resulting divorce decree is *ex parte*. In general, states will not recognize ex parte divorce decrees, unless the absent party has received proper notice. If the absent spouse receives proper notice and appears in the case, either in person or through an attorney, the divorce decree is considered *bilateral*. Some states will be satisfied with a foreign divorce order if this requirement has been met.

Estoppel

If an absent spouse agrees to the foreign divorce, or somehow benefits from the other spouse getting the divorce in another country—for example, by remarrying in reliance on the foreign dissolution—then the absent spouse will be barred from challenging the validity of the foreign divorce at another time. Stopping a party, who at first went along with and benefited from the process, from complaining about it later is called *estoppel*.

Custody, Alimony, and Division of Property

Keep in mind that, even if you properly serve your spouse with notice of your pending foreign divorce and he or she goes along with it, and even if he or she decides to accompany you to the foreign jurisdiction, it is possible that all you will get is a simple divorce. Although your home state may recognize a foreign quickie divorce, it may be the case that any alimony or division of property provisions—which many foreign courts will not order in any event—will not be recognized by certain state courts in the United States. In other states, the court will recognize the divorce order, but will not enforce any support or property division rulings. This means that even though a court may rule that the divorce is valid and therefore may not be re-litigated in the United States, the court will not allow a party to use the American legal system to force the other party to comply with the order. In such a case, the party seeking enforcement would have to return to the foreign court for assistance.

Moreover, custody orders entered in a foreign country are subject to special scrutiny in the United States. All states, for example, regulate custody according to certain uniform laws in order to prevent a parent from kidnapping the children. States will also generally require that custody determinations are based on the best interests of the child. It is unlikely that a state will give up jurisdiction over children whose custody is governed by one of the uniform laws, which are discussed in more detail in Chapter 11. It is even less likely that a state will recognize a custody order that does not account for the child's best interests.

If maintenance and property division are not issues for you or your spouse, either because you have settled the question already or because there is no money or property to haggle over, it is possible that a foreign divorce will be sufficient. Otherwise, you may have to return to court in the United States after obtaining the foreign decree, to allow the state court to iron out any remaining maintenance or property division questions.

Several federal and uniform laws have been formulated that deal with foreign country divorce orders, and international support or custody orders in particular. They include:

- Uniform Interstate Family Support Act;
- Uniform Foreign Money Judgments Recognition Act;
- Parental Kidnapping Prevention Act (federal); and,
- Uniform Child Custody Jurisdiction Act/Uniform Child Custody Jurisdiction and Enforcement Act.

In some states, the uniform Acts cover enforcement of foreign country divorce judgments. However, in other states, the Acts may specifically exclude foreign country divorce judgments. You should check your state's most recent statutory code to see which of these statutes is currently in force.

The bottom line is that cases are very fact-specific when it comes to domestic courts deciding whether to give effect to a divorce granted in another country. Two situations may have similar facts, but even a slight difference may make a prior decision unreliable as precedent in a later case. The United States State Department recommends that someone with a question as to the validity of a foreign divorce contact the attorney general of his or her home state for guidance.

CHAPTER 8:
Uncontested Divorces

What follows in this chapter is the key to a true quickie divorce: cooperation between the parties. For those seeking a rapid end to their marriage, a noncombative divorce is probably the best bet. An uncontested, or *summary*, divorce is one in which the respondent spouse receives proper service of process, and either fails to file an answer or appear in court, or files an answer in which he or she does not dispute the petitioner's allegations. To obtain a summary divorce by agreement, you and your spouse must reach an agreement on every single issue in the case: custody and visitation, if you have minor children; division of marital property and allocation of marital debt; and maintenance, if any is sought by either party. Truth be told, the majority of divorce cases eventually are resolved by the parties finding a way to agree, whether it is before or after the filing of the actual petition for dissolution.

Default Judgment

Of course, another way of obtaining an uncontested divorce is if your spouse, after being properly served with process, simply decides not to appear in court or respond to your petition. Such a failure to appear will lead to a *default judgment* being entered in your favor on all issues. In reality, however, this is unlikely to happen.

Even if your spouse does say he or she will not be answering your dissolution petition, there is no guarantee that you will end up with a judgment by default. Your spouse may decide to show up at the last minute to contest the petition or may send an attorney. In the rare case in which the respondent does not appear and the court grants a default judgment, it may not be in place for long. Courts routinely *vacate*, or cancel, default judgments if the respondent makes a motion to vacate within a certain time after the default order is entered. Typically, a default can be vacated within thirty days of its entry, but judges often will vacate even after a longer period of time, if the respondent has shown good cause for failing to appear earlier. This is because a divorce decree is a final resolution of a number of very important matters for both parties. Courts are very hesitant to do this without giving both sides every possible opportunity to be heard.

Unless you have a spouse who has a very good reason not to appear before a judge, you should not count on obtaining a default judgment. You are far more likely to obtain a fast termination to your marriage if you and your spouse are able to work out an amicable settlement of the issues at stake in your divorce case.

Mediation

Mediation is a voluntary, cooperative process of problem-solving between the parties to a divorce. Both parties must agree to and desire to participate in mediation for it to work. Both parties also must agree to make full disclosure of all matters that are subject to mediation. For the most part, states require disclosures made in mediation to remain confidential. In case your state does not require confidentiality, you should insist on a separate, written confidentiality agreement between you, your spouse, and the mediator.

When a couple goes the route of mediation, the atmosphere and procedures are completely different from when you go to court. When you go to court, the parties each have a representative who attempts to win as much as possible for his or her client. This is called a "win-lose" situation. In mediation, however, the mediator works with both sides in order to come up with a resolution that is satisfactory to both sides. That is a "win-win" scenario. The parties tend to be happier with the result of mediation, and when the agreement is incorporated into the divorce decree, the parties are usually much less likely to go back to court later in order to change the terms of the divorces. In turn, the entire divorce process ends up taking less time, effort, and money than in the traditional litigation process.

The usual mediation procedure involves a number of sessions with a professional mediator who has been fully trained in dispute resolution. Often, the mediator is a licensed attorney, but he or she may also be a psychologist or other mental health professional. The mediator must remain neutral at all times during the process. He or she may not take sides and may not give advice to one side or the other. Either type of conduct would diminish the credibility of the mediator. If, at any time during the process, a party feels that he or she should have legal representation, it is perfectly acceptable to have the party's own attorney present during any of the sessions.

Initial Mediation Session

It is common to use an initial session to explain the mediation process to the parties and to talk about the issues that might be sources of contention in the case. That way, the focus of the discussions can be narrowed to those topics that truly may cause conflict.

EXAMPLE:

Ronald and Mary are perfectly happy to waive maintenance in their divorce, because both have high-paying jobs and neither feels entitled to anything more from the other spouse. What both of them really want, however, is title to the vacation condo in the Caribbean that they own jointly. At an initial session, the mediator can cross the issue of maintenance right off the list of topics to be settled, leaving more time to concentrate on the real source of strife for the couple.

In general, the issues in need of mediation for most couples can be placed in one of four categories: child custody, child support, property division, and maintenance. Within each category are any number of problems and sub-issues. Take custody, for example. Even if the parties agree that the wife should have primary physical residential custody of the children, they also have to agree on the days when the husband has the children. They also must reach common ground on questions such as grandparent visitation, who has the authority to make what decisions on behalf of the children, what religion the children will follow, and on and on. Each sub-question will require cooperation and reasonableness from both sides if they are to avoid a costly and lengthy court case.

The other purpose of an initial session is to discuss documents that the parties need to gather for the next session. The list usually is similar to what is necessary for preparing a case for litigation and includes:

- paycheck stubs and W-2 forms;
- tax returns;
- bank and other financial statements;
- mortgage documents;
- deeds and bills of sale relating to personal property;
- insurance policies; and,
- similar documents relating to businesses owned by one or both parties.

Other requested documents might relate to the parties' children, such as information regarding school and extracurricular activities, medical or mental health information, and so on.

The Mediator

In order to achieve a win-win outcome, the mediator has to treat each side's position as important and worth hearing. Oftentimes, the emotional issues outweigh any of the tangible points at stake in the case. A good mediator will be empathetic to both sides, no matter how obvious it may seem that one side is at fault and one is innocent. The mediator also must encourage the parties to work together, so that they both are invested in the process. This way, both sides will be more likely to live up to the terms of the marital settlement and eventual divorce decree. This, in turn, will help keep the parties out of court post-divorce.

The mediator's job is to facilitate the parties in reaching an agreement. This is accomplished by helping the couple explore the various options available for resolving the couple's differences. First, each party decides which alternatives are out of the question. Then, the mediator goes through all of the remaining choices with the couple to see which ones might be used to come to an agreement. The idea is to help each party find the items that he or she can be flexible with. By allowing some "give" on those points, the party hopefully can trade off for another item on which he or she is not so willing to be flexible.

EXAMPLE:

Joan wants the couple's collection of antiques, but does not feel so strongly about keeping their fishing boat, so this might be a good spot to negotiate for the item she wants by allowing Mark to have something that is of little importance to her. Contrast that with the adversarial scenario of litigation. There, Joan digs in her heels to keep the fishing boat, not because she wants it, but because she does not want Mark to have it. Joan can spend a great deal of time and money having her attorney press the case for the boat, when all she really wants is the antique collection. By working on each separate point of contention one step at a time, the mediator can guide the parties toward a deal that both sides can live with.

The End Product

Once the mediator and the couples have come up with an agreement on all of the points that were in dispute at the beginning of mediation, the draft agreement is prepared. The mediator, one of the attorneys, or one of the parties may prepare the draft. This is not the final agreement, but a first copy that the parties then can bring to their respective attorneys to review. It is a good idea to have someone with tax expertise look over the agreement so that you understand the tax implications of the contract.

After the draft is reviewed, and any changes proposed by the parties are agreed to and incorporated, both parties will sign the final agreement. Then one or both of the parties present the final agreement to the court for approval. If the court is satisfied with the terms, it will include them in the dissolution decree.

Collaborative Divorce

Related to the purposes and processes of mediation is a recent trend in divorce law known as *collaborative divorce*. This is a method by which the parties work together, assisted by their attorneys, to reach agreement before a divorce action is even commenced. Collaboration differs from mediation in that, while mediation is led by one neutral third-party mediator, the collaborative process involves four points of view—each party and each attorney.

Unlike mediation, where the professional in charge is impartial, the lawyers in collaborative divorce are advocates for their respective clients. That is not to say they are adversarial; on the contrary, collaborative lawyers have received training in the problem-solving process. Not only that, the parties and the lawyers usually sign an agreement before starting the problem-solving process. In this contract, the parties agree that, if the collaboration breaks down and the case goes to litigation, the attorneys will withdraw and the parties will retain other counsel to represent them.

In the collaborative field, a couple may have additional personnel to assist the process. Sometimes, a financial specialist may be enlisted to give advice on the economic consequences of various settlement options in the divorce case. A mental health specialist also may be present to assist with the emotional aspects of the divorce. It makes sense to have this additional support along with the legal representation. The financial and emotional factors in a divorce case are almost always what causes conflict. If the parties have extra help in these areas, hopefully the parties will have a better mindset for coming to a win-win resolution in their divorce.

When Collaboration Is Not an Option

If collaborative divorce is such a fast and cost-effective method for reaching an agreeable marital settlement, shouldn't everyone go that route? Unfortunately, the answer is no.

The key to success in collaboration is trust. If parties are extremely angry at each other, if one party has been very controlling in the past, or if either spouse believes the other spouse is dishonest or untrustworthy, then collaborative divorce probably is not the best option. Although some collaborative law experts insist that high-conflict couples can benefit from the process, there may be many obstacles to a win-win resolution in such a case.

In a collaborative divorce, both parties are expected to provide full and complete disclosure of all assets. Usually, they both have signed an agreement that requires them to make such disclosures.

EXAMPLE:

Midge believes that Sam, a small business owner, is hiding some of his company's annual profit. She feels like she will be a sucker if she sits through the collaboration sessions, where she is expected to problem-solve and compromise. She becomes resentful of Sam, as well as his attorney, and believes she is being taken advantage of for trying to reach an amicable settlement. Before long, she will probably back out of the collaboration and hire an adversarial attorney to conduct all kinds of discovery and obtain a favorable property distribution for her. As a result, all that Midge and Sam have done is delay the divorce because of the wasted time in collaboration.

The lesson from this example is that, if you do not trust your spouse, and you doubt his or her honesty, you may be better off with a traditional litigated divorce, and all of the discovery tools that come with it.

Aside from the money- and time-saving advantages of an agreed-upon divorce decree, there is one benefit that overrides the others: the effect the process has upon your children, if you have any. As opposed to a litigated divorce, a mediated or collaborative dissolution should produce less conflict. This, in turn, will show your children that *both* parents have integrity, and will keep your kids' interests at the forefront.

CHAPTER 9:
Property Settlement

Next to child custody issues, nothing causes more contention in divorce cases than the division of marital assets and debts between the parties. Otherwise calm, rational people can dig their heels in over the most insignificant items of personal property, things they do not even want. The personal property comes to represent a means of exacting retribution for all of the wrongs a party feels he or she has suffered at the hands of the other spouse.

Of course, the more combative the dealings are with regard to the marital property, the more time it will take to reach the final divorce decree. With that in mind, it is important for you to decide what property you truly want, and which items you are willing to part with for the sake of speeding up the process. Most couples are able to reach agreement on property division issues on their own—or with the help of attorneys or mediators—and can avoid having to litigate the matters before a judge. You and your spouse will need to determine whether the property you both own is worth holding up the progress of your case.

Division of Property

State statutes regulate how a couple's property is divided in dissolution. In general, the question is whether a particular item is *marital property* or *separate property*. Marital property is that which belongs to the couple jointly. This property is what is split up between the spouses according to the division rules in the jurisdiction. Separate property belongs to only one of the spouses, and will remain the property of that party at the time of the final divorce decree. Courts in most states have held that assets acquired by one party after the time a petition for dissolution has been filed are to be considered that party's separate property.

How does the court determine what is marital property and what is separate? The basic rule is that property acquired during the marriage by either party is marital property. The two main exceptions are property acquired by one of the parties by either gift or inheritance. Some states have ruled that the payment of a personal injury judgment to one of the spouses also is separate property. In general, property belonging to one of the parties prior to the marriage is considered separate property. However, under some circumstances, separate property can be converted into marital property. There are exceptions to these general rules; Appendix B provides an overview of these exceptions.

If the spouse who owns the separate property makes what is considered a *gift to the marriage*, the property becomes marital property subject to equitable distribution.

EXAMPLE:

Morris inherits $20,000 from his deceased aunt. At the moment he receives it, the money would be separate property. However, Morris uses the money to remodel the kitchen of his home, which he and his wife, Rhonda, own together. The home had a fair market value of $275,000 prior to the remodel; afterward, the home is worth $290,000. The $15,000 increase in the value of the real estate is considered a gift to the marital partnership, is now owned by both Morris and Rhonda, and can be divided between them if they ever divorce.

Various state courts have held the following items, among others, to be marital property:

- each party's earnings during the marriage;
- pension plans;
- professional (law or medical) licenses;
- a master's degree; and,
- lottery prizes when tickets were purchased with marital property.

Typically, any property that is acquired by using the proceeds from marital property will itself be marital property.

States fall into one of two categories with regard to the manner of dividing property: *equitable distribution* and *community property*. The state-by-state analysis of each jurisdiction in Appendix B indicates which jurisdictions use which method of division.

Equitable Distribution

In an equitable distribution state, the idea is that property will be split up in a fair way, as dictated by a number of factors the court considers. Note that *equitable* does not necessarily mean *equal*. The court's job is to make a division of the couple's assets, with one spouse perhaps receiving more or less than half based upon the statutory considerations of the particular state's law.

Courts will consider some or all of the following factors in determining how to equitably divide the couple's property:

- the length of the marriage;
- the ages and health of the parties;
- each party's economic condition at the time the settlement would be valid;

- the economic and/or domestic contribution of each party to the marriage, including contributions leading to the obtaining or appreciation in value of property;
- a party's contribution to the education and/or career of the other party;
- the future employability of each party;
- the conduct of each party during the marriage;
- any attempts to dissipate marital property;
- the terms of any prenuptial agreement between the parties;
- the needs of any minor children of the marriage;
- the custody arrangement of any minor children;
- any support obligations of either party due to a previous marriage;
- the tax consequences of the property division;
- whether either party has unvested pension rights;
- whether one party, having custody of a minor child of the marriage, needs possession of the marital home; and,
- such other factors that the court finds relevant.

You may believe that your spouse's fault in the breakup of the marriage entitles you to a greater share of the marital estate. However, in most cases this is not true. Usually, *marital misconduct* is not actually considered when the court is dividing up marital property. The exception to this is in the case where the spouse's misconduct serves to hide or deplete marital assets. In that event, the court may order a division of property that favors the spouse who did not commit the wrong.

Community Property

Nine states—Arizona, California, Idaho, Louisiana, Nevada, New Mexico, Texas, Washington, and Wisconsin—are *community property* states. This means that, in these jurisdictions, all property acquired during the marriage belongs to the marital partnership. In some community property jurisdictions, that even includes assets acquired by gift or inheritance. Without an agreement that says something else, all community property is divided equally between the two parties. Even if a couple has lived in an equitable distribution state and acquired most of their assets there, if they move to a community property state, the court will treat all of the assets as community property for the purposes of property division.

Allocation of Debts

Liabilities also need to be divided between the parties. However, creditors of the parties are not bound by orders of a divorce that relieve one of the parties of a debt. Therefore, even if your divorce decree says your spouse is responsible for the outstanding balance of your joint credit card account, if he or she does not pay, the credit card company still can come after you for the entire amount due. For that reason, it is advisable for anyone considering filing for a divorce or legal separation to close out all charge card accounts and equity lines of credit as soon as possible. You also should give notice to all joint creditors, in writing, that you will take no further responsibility for any new debt on any accounts as of the date of the notice.

As a general rule, one spouse may not argue that he or she is not responsible for a debt that he or she knew nothing about. However, courts can ascribe debt to one spouse if he or she intentionally incurred it in order to keep assets from the other spouse, particularly in a case where marital misconduct is involved.

EXAMPLE:

Jim purchases a family burial plot without telling Lisa. Lisa cannot claim in the divorce that the bill for the plot should be allocated to Jim. On the other hand, if Jim purchases a weekend getaway with his mistress, the court would be able to allocate that debt solely to Jim.

Tax Issues in Property Division

Tax considerations connected with marital property distributions can be complex and far-reaching. A thorough discussion of tax issues resulting from dissolution of marriage is beyond the scope of this book. Therefore, you would be well advised to speak to an attorney with a high level of experience with taxation in divorce. In order to help you understand some of the tax ramifications of distributing property during dissolution proceedings, the Internal Revenue Service offers its Publication 504, *Divorced or Separated Individuals*. This publication can be found online at **www.irs.gov**, or can be ordered for mail delivery by calling 800-829-3676.

Under normal circumstances, if a taxpayer transfers property to another person and receives a financial gain on the transaction, the taxpayer is liable for tax on that gain. The general rule is that no gain or loss occurs when a transfer is made from one spouse to another pursuant to a divorce proceeding. This means that the transfer of assets must either be because of the divorce or must take place within one year after the divorce decree. There are a few limited exceptions where gain on such a transfer is taxable, such as a transfer to a spouse who is a nonresident alien.

If you live in a community property state, note that distinct tax rules will apply. Community income, including earnings paid to you and your spouse while you are still married, is taxed one-half to each spouse during the marriage. At the point where the marriage ends, earnings of each spouse become separate income. The income then is taxed separately to each spouse, according to who earned it. Again, because tax law connected with divorce in community property states is so complicated, someone going through a divorce in one of those jurisdictions should discuss tax implications with an experienced attorney. The Internal Revenue Service also has a booklet discussing these issues—Publication 555, *Community Property*.

The distribution of marital property, if contested, can turn out to be one of the most contentious parts of the divorce process. If you are looking to complete your divorce action as quickly as possible, here is one place where you can save time. Of course, if your spouse chooses not to be reasonable, then you will have to decide whether you value the speed of the divorce or the quality of your property settlement. Be aware of the possibility that your spouse could take advantage of your desire to be done with the marriage quickly. He or she could use the litigation itself as a bargaining chip in order to obtain more than his or her fair share of the marital estate.

EXAMPLE:

Clark wants to be divorced as soon as possible in order to marry his new girlfriend, and he is willing to give Judy a bigger share of the marital property to keep her from dragging out the court case. If Judy realizes that she has the upper hand here, she may hold the prospect of dragged-out litigation over Clark's head in order to get more of the property. Clark does not care about the personal property at the time, but if his new relationship goes sour, he may realize too late that he gave away too much for that quick divorce.

CHAPTER 10:
Spousal Support

Maintenance, sometimes referred to as *alimony*, is monetary support that the court orders one spouse to pay to the other pursuant to the divorce. In many families, one spouse puts on hold his or her outside career, and the earning power that goes with it, in order to support the other spouse or to raise children.

Typically, *maintenance* falls into one of two or three categories: temporary, permanent, and sometimes rehabilitative. Temporary and rehabilitative maintenance are much more common than permanent maintenance these days. The goal of ordering maintenance is to allow the recipient to obtain or regain employment skills that may have been lacking because of time out of the workplace.

Most states have an objective formula that courts use to calculate child support obligations. In contrast, however, most states' methods of figuring out whether to order maintenance and if so, how much and for how long, are based on a number of subjective factors. In general, some of the considerations involved are similar to what the courts look at in determining how to divide marital property:

- the length of the marriage;
- the standard of living achieved during the marriage;
- the age and health of the party requesting maintenance;
- each party's economic condition at the time the marriage is dissolved;
- the future employability of each party, including the cost of and time required for adequate education of the requesting spouse, and the ability of the respondent spouse to make maintenance payments for the duration of the court's order; and,
- such other factors that the court finds relevant.

In many cases, it seems clear who is entitled to maintenance. If the standard of living is high, and the income of one of the spouses is low or nonexistent, as in the case of a stay-at-home mom, it is likely that the court will order some amount of maintenance, at least until the divorce decree is entered. Sometimes, however, it is not so obvious who should pay support to whom. As a result, there may be more than one hearing on the issue of maintenance: one early on to fix temporary alimony, and one to determine the final maintenance payment schedule.

If you wish to request maintenance in your case, you will need to file a motion for temporary support with the court. If your spouse is seeking maintenance and you want to dispute his or her claim, you will need to contest the motion. In such a case, the judge probably will order an *evidentiary hearing*. This is where it is important to have done your information gathering, as discussed in Chapter 4. You will need to show evidence not only of your income and other financial resources, but those of your spouse as well.

Temporary Maintenance

Maintenance that is awarded only for the duration of the actual divorce proceeding, until the final decree is entered, is known as *temporary maintenance*. In some jurisdictions, it is called alimony *pendente lite*, or alimony while the litigation is pending.

As with other temporary rulings in divorce court, once the amount of alimony is fixed on a temporary basis, it is likely that the court will stick with the figure already in place, or very near it.

EXAMPLE:

The judge orders John to pay Jill maintenance in the amount of $300 per month until the final divorce decree is entered. The final order is likely to provide for about the same monthly amount. If the court had a compelling reason to award more maintenance, it probably would have done so in the temporary alimony ruling.

Rehabilitative Maintenance

Some jurisdictions use the terms *temporary maintenance* and *rehabilitative maintenance* interchangeably. They are discussed here separately, however, because some states have a special category of maintenance that is meant either to restore a spouse to his or her former career level, or to help the spouse receive job training for a new career. Usually, the right to *rehabilitative maintenance* goes to the spouse who has sacrificed his or her education or career for the sake of the marriage and family, with the result that he or she has been unemployed or underemployed over several years.

Courts usually do not order rehabilitative maintenance on a long-term basis. It is meant as a means to put the recipient spouse in the position he or she would have been in had the spouse not given up employment or educational opportunities in order to put the marriage and home on the front burner. Some state statutes, in fact, expressly limit the length of time for which rehabilitative maintenance is allowed. For example, Indiana law provides that the court may order rehabilitative maintenance for no longer than three years.

Permanent Maintenance

Maintenance that is ordered in a final decree but does not have a definite end date is considered *permanent maintenance*. The trend in most states nowadays is to not award permanent maintenance unless there is a compelling reason for it. That case would usually involve a couple who have been married for a very long time, or a recipient spouse who has a very limited ability to become self-supporting, such as someone with a debilitating illness.

Although it is referred to as permanent, this type of maintenance does not necessarily go on indefinitely. Courts usually will include a provision in the decree that allows termination of the maintenance in the case of certain events. Typically, these will include the following:

- death of either spouse;
- remarriage of the recipient spouse; or,
- cohabitation of the recipient spouse with another of the opposite sex.

Lump-Sum Payment

Some jurisdictions will consider agreements between the parties for one spouse to pay alimony in the form of a single lump-sum payment rather than a periodic payment over a number of months or years. The advantage of this arrangement to the recipient, obviously, is that he or she gets the money quickly and up front. The incentive for a spouse who has to pay the support to enter into this type of agreement is that he or she is relieved from the continued burden of making payments. That spouse usually will require, in exchange for the advance payment, that the recipient spouse sign a waiver giving up the right to return to court at a later date to request an increase in the amount or duration of alimony. That spouse, in turn, also may be required to waive the right to request a refund of any of the payment at a later date. Lump-sum payments may turn out to be disadvantageous to one or the other of the parties. A change in circumstances after the agreed amount is paid and waivers have been given could make the lump-sum arrangement a bad deal.

EXAMPLE:

Frank gives Susan $100,000 as a lump-sum maintenance payment in 2007, but then loses his job in 2008. Frank is out all of that money and has given up the ability to ask that his financial obligation be decreased.

Of course, the opposite situation could also happen. The spouse who receives the lump-sum payment might experience a change in circumstances that would have allowed him or her to have received an increase in payments in a traditional arrangement. Changes in maintenance orders are discussed in Chapter 14. Consider these possibilities carefully if you are thinking about agreeing to a lump-sum maintenance payment.

Tax Issues Connected to Maintenance

For taxes, the bottom line of maintenance is this: alimony payments deductible by the payor spouse and taxable as income to the recipient spouse. In particular, according to the Internal Revenue Service, each of the following are required for this rule to apply:

- the parties may not file a joint tax return together;
- payments must be made in cash or the equivalent;
- there must not be anything in the divorce decree or separation agreement that says the payment is not alimony;
- the parties may not be living in the same household at the time of the payment;
- the payments are not considered to be for child support; and,
- the payor spouse is no longer obligated for the payments once the recipient spouse dies.

Cash or the equivalent means checks, money orders, or certain payments to third parties on behalf of the recipient. For example, a payment made by the payor spouse for the recipient spouse's medical expenses can be deducted as alimony. On the other hand, a transfer of property from the payor to the recipient would not be considered maintenance for tax purposes.

Each spouse must include the other spouse's Social Security number on his or her tax return in order for the payor to claim the deduction. If either party fails to do this, the Internal Revenue Service can assess a $50 penalty against that party.

Qualified Domestic Relations Orders

A term you are likely to hear during the course of your divorce is *QDRO* (pronounced *quadro*). A *qualified domestic relations order* (QDRO) is a court order that concerns a spouse's right to receive benefits under the other spouse's pension, profit-sharing, or other qualified retirement plan. Another requirement for an order to be a QDRO is that it concerns payment of maintenance, child support, or property rights to the participant's spouse or children. The general rule is that plan payments made to the participant's spouse are to be included in the spouse's income.

Individual Retirement Accounts

Another common tax issue in divorce arises with regard to an individual retirement account belonging to one of the spouses. An *individual retirement account* (IRA) is a retirement investment fund to which a person contributes part of his or her income on an annual basis. The income that is set aside generally is not taxable. If your separation agreement or decree of dissolution orders you to transfer an interest in an IRA to your spouse, the transfer of the IRA is not taxable as income.

CHAPTER 11:
Considerations for Couples with Children

Although nothing is guaranteed in divorce court, one thing comes close: almost any case involving minor children is going to take longer for a divorce decree than a case without children. Even if you and your spouse are in complete agreement on such issues as child support, child custody, or visitation, the court is likely to take a closer look at the parties' agreement with regard to these than it would in the case of strictly financial considerations, such as maintenance and property division. The reason, of course, is that the well-being of minor children during the divorce process is of utmost importance to the court.

Child Support

A couple's minor child has the right to be supported financially. As a result, parents are not allowed to agree between themselves that one will be relieved of the duty to pay child support in return for signing away rights to custody or visitation. If one parent was allowed to negotiate away the duty to support, and the other parent then became disabled and could not meet the child's needs, the child could end up in the welfare system. In such a case, the government, using funds collected from taxpayers, would become responsible for supporting the child. By prohibiting agreements to relieve one parent of his or her legal obligation, states try to avoid unnecessary placement of children on the welfare rolls. For the same reason, parties may not agree to make child support non-modifiable.

A parent's right to visitation is separate from the duty to support. If one parent is not contributing to the child's support, the custodial parent may not refuse to allow visitation. However, the failure to pay support may be one factor that impacts the best interests of the child. As such, it may be considered by a court in determining the parties' respective custody or visitation rights.

Both parents have a duty to financially support their child. If one parent is providing more than his or her fair share of the money to pay for the child's necessities, that parent can petition the court to order the other parent to contribute. This is the case whether the parties are seeking divorce or annulment, were never married, or even if they are not separating at all.

Amount and Duration of Support Payments

In most states, the legislature has provided statutory guidelines for determining the proper amount of support for which each parent is responsible. This is the starting point for any discussion of child support. Support often is ordered to be paid out of the income of the paying parent, although, as discussed later, support may come from the assets of his or her estate.

When one parent's income differs greatly from one year to the next, the court may average the parent's income over several prior years to determine his or her income level. If the court is not able to determine a parent's net income, for example, because the parent has failed to file a financial affidavit or a response to a request by the other party for support, then the court is authorized to order an amount of support considered reasonable in the particular case.

Courts generally are required to follow guidelines unless the court finds that doing so would not be in the best interest of the child. In making such a finding, the court should consider all relevant factors, such as the financial needs and resources of each parent and the children, the physical and emotional condition of each parent and each child; the family's standard of living before the marriage ended; and, the educational and medical needs of each child.

A party asking the court for a deviation from the guidelines has the burden of convincing the court to disregard the statute. Oftentimes, the statute of the particular state requires the court to make written findings setting out the reasons for the deviation. In some states, a payor spouse with an income over a certain amount is not covered by the guideline amounts; the court may set an amount that is commensurate with the income level. Typical causes of departure from the guidelines are:

- one parent has custody of the children, and the other parent has less than the statutory standard amount of visitation;
- both parents have shared custody, so that adherence to the guidelines would cause duplication of support;
- one parent is mainly responsible for substantial travel expenses related to visitation; or,
- the child has his or her own assets or unearned income.

Some states do not give specific reasons for a court to depart from the terms of the statute. Rather, they rely on standards such as what is in the best interests of the child in determining what amount of child support is appropriate. However, be sure to check the statutes and case law of your state to see what the rules are for deviation from the jurisdiction's guidelines.

Tax Considerations

As with any financial concern that arises in a divorce context, child support arrangements may present various tax issues that need to be addressed. The general rule is fairly straightforward: payments made for child support are not deductible by the payor spouse, and are not taxable income to the recipient spouse. What sometimes gets sticky is determining what constitutes child support in the first place.

Keep in mind that a thorough treatment of tax law relating to child support is beyond the scope of this book. Usually, the best course of action in child support cases where tax concerns come up is to consult with an attorney who has experience in this area. In addition, the Internal Revenue Service has publications that might provide some useful information. IRS Publication 504, *Divorced or Separated Individuals*, discusses claiming minor children as dependents, among other topics. Publication 4449, *Tax Information for Non-Custodial Parents*, covers other subjects such as the earned income and dependent care tax credits. Both publications can be found online at **www.irs.gov**.

Custody and Visitation

The terms *custody* and *visitation* refer to a collection of rights and responsibilities held by a person with regard to certain minor children. Usually, this person is one of the parents of the children, but under certain circumstances, other parties may receive custodial or visitation rights. Most often, the nonparent seeking custody or visitation is a grandparent or stepparent. You should be familiar with several types of custody, discussed in the following sections.

Physical and Legal Custody

Physical custody refers to both the actual possession and the physical control of the child. *Legal custody*, on the other hand, is the power to make decisions on behalf of the child, such as his or her education, activities, and religious upbringing. Both types of custody may be vested in a single person, or the rights and responsibilities may be divided between the parents as the court sees fit. Custody determinations are made according to the best interests of the child standard, which is discussed on page 88.

Joint Custody

A court may make an award of joint custody; in fact, in many jurisdictions, it is the stated goal that joint custody be awarded to the parents whenever possible. In general, this means that both physical and legal custody is divided between both parents. Again, joint custody must be in the best interests of the child. The court will take into account, among other factors, whether the parents are able to cooperate in matters covered by the court's joint parenting order.

Note, however, that this does not necessarily mean that each parent will have equal time with the child. One parent may be given primary residential custody of the child in a joint parenting situation, with the other parent receiving less amount of contact.

Temporary Custody

If there are minor children involved in your divorce, and you have not agreed with your spouse ahead of time as to how custody is to be split between you, there usually will be a court order assigning temporary custody while the case is pending. *Temporary custody*, true to its name, is not the final determination of the rights and responsibilities at issue. Keep in mind, however, that courts often end up continuing provisions of a temporary custody order when the final custody determination is made.

EXAMPLE:

Lois and Blaine have filed for divorce. Lois is awarded temporary physical custody, so that their child spends only every other weekend with Blaine. If the case goes on for a year before a final decree is entered, the court is more likely to simply leave the custody arrangement as it is rather than to give the father more access to the child at the time of the final award of custody. Because the child now has spent many months in this living situation, the court will hesitate to disturb the child's routine after the passage of so much time, unless there is a very good reason for doing so.

This means that it is important to obtain a favorable temporary custody award as early as possible, as the provisions of the temporary order may end up carrying over to the final custody award.

Best Interests of the Child

In making a determination of custody, courts will look to the *best interests of the child*. The standard is not actually defined, but generally, it refers to the situation that is most beneficial to the child, in light of the fact that the child's parents are no longer together. In some states, the best interests of the child standard is set out by statute, with definite factors listed for a court to refer to in making a decision. Some of these factors are explained here.

Wishes of the Parents

Although important, the parents' wishes as to who receives custody are not the only factor considered in making the custody determination. Too often, a parent will seek custody for reasons other than what is best for the child. Some parents may be motivated by a desire for revenge against the other parent. Others may petition for custody in the hope that they can bargain for a smaller spousal or child support obligation. Courts, therefore, will consider the parents' wishes, but generally will not base an award of custody on those wishes without other evidence of the child's best interest, unless the parents fully agree on how custody should be split up.

Wishes of the Child

A court sometimes will ask the child with which parent he or she prefers to live. Whether the court does inquire, however, and the amount of weight the court will give to the child's preference, will depend on the age and maturity level of the child. Children under the age of 8 usually will not be consulted about their choice of custodial parent. On the other hand, courts often give considerable weight to the wishes of children aged 14 and above. Remember, though, that the child's preference should be based on his or her relationship with the parent. His or her stated preference should not be grounded on some other factor, such as the child's desire to remain near his or her friends.

Interaction and Interrelationship

The interaction and interrelationship factors refer to the relationships between the child and those people who have important interactions with the child. Most often, that means members of the child's family, but can include anyone who materially impacts the child's best interests. The court will look at the way in which a particular custody award might affect these relationships.

Child's Adjustment

In general, the child's adjustment refers to how the child is faring in the most important parts of his or her environment—home, school, and community. One example would be the case in which both the mother and the father are deemed good parents, but the mother has been the primary caregiver for the child's whole life and the father has spent long hours at work and much of his time at home working as well. In such a case, custody may very well end up going to the mother. In one real-life case, the instability of the child's home life was considered in a situation where the mother left the father, removing the children from the marital home without informing the father. Soon thereafter, the mother moved the children again, and within the year, moved yet a third time. Custody in that case was awarded to the father.

Mental and Physical Health of All Involved

The mental and physical health of not only the child, but also those others who live in the home or who have similarly close and substantial contact with the child, such as extended family members, is considered. This consideration includes both the medical and the emotional state of each of these people. A court will not remove a child from the custody of a parent with a disability so long as the best interests of the child is not affected.

Physical Violence or Abuse

Prior physical violence, or the threat of violence, by the person seeking custody, no matter if it is directed toward the child or toward someone else, is going to have great impact on the court's decision on the child's best interests. *Abuse* includes physical violence, but also encompasses harassment and intimidation by the person seeking custody. This abuse may be directed at *any* person, not just the child, for the court to consider the effect of the petitioning parent's conduct on the best interests of the child.

Relationship with Other Parent

The likelihood that each parent will encourage the relationship between the child and the other parent is also often a factor. Attempts by one parent to turn the child against the other parent, or to interfere with the other parent's contact with the child, are against the best interests of the child.

Other Factors

Courts and statutes have delineated a number of other circumstances to examine in determining the best interest of the child. Among these are:

- false allegations by one parent of abuse by the other parent;
- substance abuse by one parent;
- failure of one parent to pay financial support for the child's benefit;
- willingness of one parent to have medical or educational issues of the child corrected;
- recommendations by a guardian ad litem appointed by the court;
- the effect of a separation of siblings;
- unauthorized attempts to move the child to another home far from the other parent;
- visitation arrangements that require excessive travel on the part of the child;
- attempts by one parent to change the last name of the child from that of the other parent; and,
- the cultural background of the child.

The remarriage of one parent is not enough by itself to count against the best interest standard, but some courts will consider a parent's sexual activity and its effect on the child. Also, one parent's wealth is not alone determinative. All relevant factors must be considered together within the context of how they impact the child's interests.

Visitation

The policy of most states is that, whenever possible, it is desirable for a child to have a relationship with both parents. To that end, a parent who is not awarded physical custody of a child is entitled to reasonable visitation with him or her unless visitation would seriously endanger the child. Therefore, denying or limiting visitation requires a more stringent showing than the best interests standard.

Courts often order what is known as *standard visitation*. Typically, the noncustodial parent has the child on alternate weekends (Friday evening to Sunday evening) and alternating holidays (for example, the mother has the child on Christmas in even-numbered years, and the father has the child on Christmas in odd-numbered years, and so on). Also, the father will have the child every year on Father's Day and the father's birthday, the mother has the child every year on Mother's Day and the mother's birthday, and the noncustodial parent has the child for approximately one-half of the child's summer vacation (four or five weeks).

The noncustodial parent can make a case for expanded visitation by providing evidence that the custodial parent is unwilling to facilitate the other parent's relationship with the child. A custodial parent's history of attempting to turn the child against the other parent, or of unreasonably refusing to allow the other parent to have contact with the child, can be viewed as a case for expanded visitation.

Savings in Support and Custody Matters

Chapter 8 deals with ways to foster agreement between parties during the divorce process, so that they can obtain an uncontested decree. Mediation is helpful for couples in high-conflict situations, but it can be useful in a case where the parties concur on most, but not all issues. A divorcing couple can undertake mediation in order to iron out just one or two sources of contention. The idea is to reach agreement and avoid the often costly and time-consuming discovery process.

Remember that, when you save time, you usually save money as well. It is true that counseling and mediation services can cost upwards of $100 per one-hour session, but an attorney for one of the parties alone typically can cost twice that. The usual mediated divorce might take ten hours or even less of mediation, while the discovery process alone in a litigated divorce can easily use up much more time than that. It becomes easy to see how mediation is a good option to explore if there are disputed items in the divorce case, such as custody, visitation, or child support.

CHAPTER 12:
Emergency Circumstances

There are some situations that may arise in the course of a divorce or separation action where time is of the essence, not only because you want the process to be over, but because there is a real danger of harm to you, your children, or your property. No matter how divorce issues are resolved, whether by court order or agreement between spouses, there is no guarantee that the other person will abide by the terms of the resolution. Discussed in this chapter are a number of situations that require an immediate response in order to prevent harm to a party, or his or her family or interests. Most states have enacted statutes to cover these types of cases. Federal law governs some of them as well.

Domestic Abuse

Domestic abuse includes the following behaviors by one family member toward another:

- physical harm or assault;
- criminal sexual conduct;
- creating fear of immediate physical harm;
- harassment or stalking;
- intimidation; and,
- neglect.

The most common relief on an emergency basis in a domestic violence case is the *emergency order of protection*. Such an order is obtained by petitioning the court, either with or without notice to the offender. The petitioner can file the petition on behalf of him- or herself, or on behalf of the minor children, or both.

Once granted, the order of protection will usually prohibit the offender from contacting any of the protected people, whether in person, by phone or fax, or otherwise. It also will stop the offender from going to places frequented by the protected parties. This includes not only the home of the protected party, but his or her workplace or school as well. Finally, the order usually will contain some language to the effect that the respondent must remain a certain distance away from the protected parties, such as five hundred feet. A copy of the order of protection should be given to the administrator of any location from which the offender is barred, such as the school office of a protected child.

An order of protection usually will not last longer than fourteen days if it was granted on an emergency basis. Once the offender has received due process—that is, notice and a court hearing—the court can grant an order of protection of a longer duration, such as twelve months.

Harassment

In some states, *harassment* is covered by a separate statute from the one addressing domestic violence. In others, it actually is considered to be a form of abuse itself. A spouse who is harassed, or caused emotional distress, by the actions of the other spouse, generally can petition a domestic violence court for relief, usually in the form of a *restraining order* or *no contact order* against the harassing spouse. Although each state's definition of harassment is different, the following examples of conduct that cause emotional distress typically are prohibited:

- appearing at the petitioner's workplace or school repeatedly, or appearing and creating a disturbance;
- stalking the petitioner;
- repeatedly telephoning the petitioner's home, school, or workplace;
- repeatedly using the mail or delivering or causing the delivery of letters, telegrams, packages, or other objects with the intent to adversely affect the safety, security, or privacy of another;
- repeatedly following the petitioner around in public;
- repeatedly threatening to use physical force against the petitioner; and,
- repeatedly threatening to remove or hide the petitioner's child.

Courts routinely will grant a temporary restraining order, even without notice having been given to the harassing party, for a short period of time, usually about seven days. To obtain an order for a longer period, you have to follow rules of due process, including notifying the other person of the petition and allowing him or her the chance to reply to the allegations of harassment.

Parental Kidnapping

Whether a parent can remove a child from his or her home state should be addressed in the final divorce decree. If a parent removes the child in violation of a custody order, the federal *Parental Kidnapping Prevention Act* (PKPA) (28 U.S.C.A. Sec. 1738A) will apply to the parent's conduct.

The PKPA states that if a custody determination was properly entered in one state, all other states must enforce that order. Once a state has taken jurisdiction over the custody matter, no other state may exercise jurisdiction at the same time. The PKPA serves to prevent one parent from removing a child from one state, where a custody order is already in place, and attempting to obtain a more favorable custody determination in another state.

In many states, a court may specifically prohibit a parent from removing a child from the court's jurisdiction, and may enter an order directing local law enforcement authorities to assist the petitioning parent in recovering the child.

Abuse of Contact or Visitation

Visitation abuse is the failure to abide by the terms of visitation set in a court order regarding custody. Sometimes, it is the parent with visitation rights who refuses to follow the court's directions, for example, by failing to return the child to the custodial parent at the designated time or place. In some cases, the parent actually may endanger the physical, emotional, or moral health of the child. Because of this possibility, courts have the right to limit visitation or require that visitation be supervised in an appropriate case. Supervision usually may be by state social service personnel, or sometimes by a third person that the court finds acceptable, such as another family member of the noncustodial parent.

Sometimes, it is the custodial parent who exercises visitation abuse. In an attempt to gain revenge on the other parent, the custodial parent will try to interfere with the other parent's access to and relationship with the child. Occasionally the interference is blatant; that is, the offending parent simply refuses to turn the child over to the other parent. More likely, however, the interference is more subtle. For example, the custodial parent will plan a fun activity, such as a trip to the amusement park, at the same time that the child is supposed to be with the other parent. The other parent then has to be the bad guy, who ruins the child's plans by insisting that the child has his or her scheduled visitation instead of going on the amusement park outing.

In such a case, the aggrieved parent can request that the court enter a *finding of contempt* against the offending parent, for the refusal to follow the court's order. The court can grant a variety of relief to the petitioner, including charging the other parent with a fine, ordering him or her to pay the petitioning parent's attorney's fees, and ordering extra makeup visitation for the petitioning parent. Unfortunately, judges sometimes do not hold parties in contempt unless the conduct is brazen or repeated. A petitioner may have to return to court a number of times before the court will find a pattern of misconduct warranting a contempt finding.

Some states provide criminal penalties for visitation interference. If you have been a victim of visitation interference, contact your local law enforcement agency to see if such conduct is unlawful in your jurisdiction. If it is, you can try to file a complaint. Even if there is no such penalty, you can ask that a police report be prepared. If the police are not cooperative, try the district attorney's office in the county in which the other parent lives. When you have a number of these incidents, the reports can help show a pattern of behavior on the part of the other spouse. Documentation of visitation interference is the best way to build a case for contempt, criminal sanctions, or other relief against the offending parent.

In a case of interference when the parties reside in different states, one of several uniform laws applies. The Uniform Child Custody Jurisdiction Act (UCCJA) and Uniform Child Custody and Jurisdiction Enforcement Act (UCCJEA) determine which state has the authority to enforce a valid visitation order. The UCCJA and UCCJEA are discussed in more detail in Chapter 13.

False Claims of Abuse

Even though most claims of domestic abuse are true, sometimes a spouse will lie about abuse in order to get revenge against the other spouse or gain an advantage in the dispute. False claims can take any number of forms. A malicious spouse may make allegations of abuse to the local district attorney or to local law enforcement officers, or may claim to the state's department of child protective services that the respondent spouse has abused the couple's children. Sometimes, a vengeful spouse will manipulate the state's social support system to get even with the other party by going from one state agency to the next with a series of untrue accusations meant to subject the other parent to the criminal justice system.

If you find yourself a victim of this tactic, the best way to protect yourself is to document, document, document. Keeping a journal with brief entries of your daily activities will help provide you with evidence to refute a false abuse claim. If the other parent accuses you of some kind of illegal conduct, such as stalking, you can reconstruct the events of that day even though you may not independently recall the date in question. A simple method of keeping track is with the use of a calendar desk pad or appointment book. Make a quick note, such as "Jamie and I baked cookies, then watched a video before bedtime." Anything that can jog your memory will be helpful if you find you have to defend yourself from a false claim.

On the other hand, if something does occur, such as Jamie tripping and skinning his knee, be careful in noting that. It may be helpful to have in writing that a minor injury happened on a particular day and how the injury occurred. Take care, however, in the event that you are ordered by the court to produce your notes. If you are the victim of a pattern of false reports, it probably is best to keep your own notes as brief as possible and try to limit them strictly to facts. This will avoid providing ammunition to the other parent who is trying to use social service and law enforcement agencies to railroad you into the position of a criminal defendant.

A number of states have legislated against false claims of abuse. Taking thorough notes of the incidents of false abuse claims can show the court a pattern of misconduct on the part of the other spouse, possibly subjecting him or her to criminal penalties of your state.

Conversion or Depletion of Marital Assets

Dissipation of marital assets occurs when one spouse, either before or during the divorce proceedings, takes action to conceal or use up marital property. This can be accomplished by removing items from the home or, in some cases, from the spouse's business so that the innocent spouse has no access to the property. Spending down bank accounts or selling marital or business property and hiding the proceeds are other methods by which marital property is drained.

The best way to protect marital property is to do so before there is a divorce situation. Removing items of personal property to a safe location before informing your spouse that you will be seeking a divorce is usually a better option than trying to recover them from his or her possession afterward. Opening a separate bank account, if you do not already have one, is also a good idea. However, take care not to remove more than your fair share of the marital property, or you may end up as the one being accused of depletion of assets.

In the event you have not already taken steps to protect your property, and you now find yourself in the position of having to safeguard your assets on an emergency basis, you may seek a protective order for the property. This will be similar to obtaining a temporary restraining order in an abuse case, in that you may appear in court on an ex parte basis, and provide notice and an opportunity for a hearing after the order is granted. Doing so will avoid tipping off your spouse that you are seeking to protect the property.

If your spouse does hide, destroy, or spend the asset before you are able to secure a protective order or in spite of an order you actually were able to obtain, the court can provide some sort of remedy after the fact. When it comes time to divide marital property in the divorce decree, the judge should take into account any assets that one party dissipated, and lessen that party's share of the marital estate by the amount wasted. Such a result can put you back in your original position monetarily; however, if the item that disappeared had sentimental value, such as a piece of heirloom jewelry from one of your relatives, the dollar value you receive in the property division may well be insufficient to make up for what you lost.

Emergency Motion for Custody

Occasionally, a parent will find him- or herself in a situation in which a child custody determination on an emergency basis is necessary. The most common case is where the custodial parent is either physically or mentally incapable of taking care of the child, or has placed the child in harm's way.

An example would be the case in which the custodial parent has been involved in an accident or become seriously ill. Such a circumstance would make it imperative that custody be changed to the noncustodial parent.

If one spouse believes that the custody issue needs to be determined on an emergency basis, the usual way to proceed is to file an emergency motion asking for immediate temporary custody. An emergency motion, as with a temporary restraining order, may be heard on an ex parte basis, without serving notice on the other party until after the hearing. It will be necessary, though, to consult the civil practice rules of your particular state and court of venue for any other procedural requirements that may exist with regard to emergency motions.

CHAPTER 13:
Enforcement of Court Orders

Obtaining the order from a judge for maintenance or child support is only part of the battle. Often, the person who is supposed to make child support or maintenance payments does not make them. In some cases, the payor spouse has a change in circumstances making it difficult to afford the payments as ordered. Sometimes, however, the payor simply refuses to pay, perhaps in retaliation for something he or she believes the recipient did, or maybe because he or she has a new family and does not feel obligated to the first family. There are not only legal procedures to assist in collecting past-due obligations, but also state administrative agencies and regulations in many jurisdictions that can aid the recipient.

Unfortunately, trying to find someone else's assets in order to satisfy a debt can prove to be a difficult, time-consuming, and frustrating process. On the upside, these are all post-divorce matters. If your goal is to end your marriage partnership, that will already have been achieved by the time you reach this stage. On the other hand, if your goal is to rid your life of your ex-spouse, enforcement proceedings likely will have the opposite result. They will cause you to spend all kinds of time not only thinking about, but also literally pursuing, your former spouse.

Child Support Enforcement

All states are required to have a system whereby child support is taken directly from the obligor's paycheck. Even if a withholding order is in place, an obligor may attempt to avoid his or her support obligation by terminating or changing his or her employment. When enforcement becomes necessary, the recipient has a number of remedies, both civil and criminal, as well as administrative.

Federal, State, and Local Enforcement Agencies

Various agencies exist at the federal and state level to assist recipients in collecting past-due child support amounts. In many states, local agencies, usually part of county government, implement the state collection programs. The purpose of these agencies is to see that parents support their children, so that taxpayers do not have to.

The U.S. Department of Health and Human Services *Office of Child Support Enforcement* (OCSE) is a federal agency that is charged with the task of locating parents who are delinquent in their payment of child support, or parents who are attempting to hide their children. The OCSE oversees the many state and local offices of child support enforcement, which do the actual enforcement operations. The OCSE was created by the same federal program that authorized states to take child support payments directly out of the obligor parents' paychecks. In some cases of families receiving public assistance, the OCSE and related state and local agencies can take past-due child support the agencies collect to reimburse the government for public assistance amounts already paid.

Suspension of State-Granted Licenses

States have begun to crack down on deadbeat parents in recent years by enacting statutes allowing the revocation of obligors' licenses. This includes driver's licenses, professional licenses, and even fishing, hunting, and boating licenses in some jurisdictions. In the case of a driver's license, typically the state can suspend the license when the obligor parent is delinquent a certain number of days on the last child support payment, and may keep it suspended until the parent is in full compliance with the support order.

Seizure of Tax Refunds

Another statutory weapon that can be used against deadbeat parents is the interception of the obligor's state and federal tax refunds. The money can be intercepted in order to pay the recipient family directly. If the family had to receive public assistance funds because of the failure to receive child support from the obligor, the seized refund money will first go to pay back the government for the assistance given. A refund may be seized to pay the government after child support arrearages reach $150, or may be taken to repay the family once the past-due amount is $500. A recent report by the U.S. Department of Health and Human Services estimated that the federal government collected more than $1.5 billion in delinquent child support in a single year by this method.

Of course, this collection method will not work if the obligor does not overpay his or her tax and, therefore, receives no refund. Also, a couple may be entitled to a refund after filing a joint tax return, but one of the spouses might owe child support to children from a prior relationship. If the entire refund is seized, even though the innocent spouse contributed income tax and should have received some of the refund, he or she would have to file a claim with the IRS as an injured spouse in order to request his or her share of the seized funds.

Notification of Credit Reporting Bureau

The federal Child Support Enforcement program allows states to notify organizations that provide credit reporting services that an obligor parent's child support payments are past due. Usually, a minimum amount must be past due, such as $500, before the nonpayment may be reported. Having a child support delinquency on one's credit report will keep that obligor from establishing credit, which in turn will impede his or her ability to purchase a car, home, or any goods on credit.

Various state child support enforcement agencies have reported that collections increase when credit reporting bureaus are notified of delinquencies. The increases generally seem to be small at the outset, but it is believed that collections will improve over time, as the delinquent obligors' credit is adversely affected.

Incarceration

Imprisonment for failure to pay child support is allowed under a couple of theories. In the first case, a court may issue what is known as a *rule to show cause*. This is an order for the obligor parent to appear before the court and explain why the court's child support ruling is not being followed. If the obligor has a legitimate reason for not paying, such as an illness that prevents him or her from holding a job, the court may not order incarceration.

If, on the other hand, the court finds that the obligor is willfully refusing to pay, or has left his or her former employment for the sole purpose of thwarting the child support order, or is hiding assets that could be used to pay support, the court may find the obligor in *contempt of court*, and may order that the obligor be remanded to custody of law enforcement until he or she complies.

The second scenario where imprisonment of a delinquent obligor is possible comes under a state or federal law, such as the *Child Support Recovery Act* (CSRA). The federal CSRA provides for federal prosecution of an out-of-state obligor with unpaid child support in excess of $5,000, or who has intentionally failed to pay support for more than one year. The burden is on the government to show that the obligor knew of the child support order and had the ability to pay, but refused to do so. The federal law is set up so that only cases in which the state remedies proved ineffective are prosecuted under the CSRA. Most states also provide for criminal penalties such as incarceration or community service for failure to pay child support.

Other Remedies

Some states have come up with a number of additional methods to obtain past-due child support. One state places photographs of the most egregious violators on billboards. Others have published lists of delinquent child support obligors in the newspaper, in the hope that the deadbeat parents will be shamed into paying what they owe. A number of states allow the confiscation of a delinquent obligor's lottery winnings. Courts also can order an obligor's employer to name the recipient child as the beneficiary of the obligor's pension plan. Finally, state child support enforcement offices can request that the U.S. State Department deny or revoke an obligor's passport if he or she is delinquent.

Out-of-State Enforcement

A number of federal and uniform state laws exist to help a recipient family collect past-due child support payments when the deadbeat parent leaves the state. The federal *Full Faith and Credit for Child Support Orders Act* (FFCCSOA) requires courts in one jurisdiction to give full faith and credit to properly entered child support orders from an out-of-state court. The *Uniform Interstate Family Support Act* (UIFSA) has been enacted by all states, and governs collection actions between states for unpaid child support. In general, the UIFSA requires that a child support order entered by a court in the child's home state takes precedence over any other support order that may have been entered elsewhere.

Spousal Support Orders

In addition to special enforcement methods for collecting delinquent child support, there are a number of traditional means that also can be used to go after unpaid maintenance. What is required first is that the past-due amount be reduced to a judgment. This means that the party asking for the enforcement has to appear in court pursuant to a motion and ask the judge to enter an order that the delinquent sum be treated as a final judgment, rather than just a claim. Once the court enters a final judgment amount, the petitioning spouse can proceed with the same collection methods that are available to anyone with a court judgment against another party, no matter what the nature of the lawsuit.

Wage Deduction and Garnishment of Assets

Now that the support arrearage has been reduced to a judgment, among the enforcement options that a petitioner can use are wage deduction and non-wage garnishment.

Wage deduction is a court-ordered withholding of a certain amount of money from each of the obligor's paychecks, until the delinquency is satisfied. The petitioner must file an action for wage deduction in the divorce case; the respondent in such a case is the obligor's employer. A *non-wage garnishment* is the taking and turning over of the obligor's property that is in the possession of a third-party respondent. An example would be a savings account held by a bank. In a non-wage garnishment, the respondent is called the *garnishee*.

In both cases, the necessary pleadings are filed and served upon the respondent, with a copy delivered to the debtor/ex-spouse as well. The respondent must answer the pleadings and then, unless there is an objection to the deduction or garnishment, must turn the money over to the petitioner. As always, check your jurisdiction's rules for any variance in these general guidelines.

Discovery of Assets/Turnover Order

Most states have a procedure by which the petitioner can enforce a judgment against the obligor's personal property through a turnover and sale. The petitioner must obtain a judgment order against specifically named personal property belonging to the deadbeat spouse. Then, the local sheriff is notified. At that point, the sheriff has the duty to confiscate and sell the obligor's property to satisfy the judgment amount. The selling of the property is known as a *sheriff's sale*.

Under certain circumstances, a court may have the authority to place some of the turned-over assets of the obligor parent into a trust for the benefit of the child. Typically, this would be ordered in the case where the obligor has engaged in some sort of fraud or other misconduct; for example, the obligor hides property or works for cash *under the table* that he or she then conceals.

Lien on Real Estate

If the parent who has to pay child support fails to pay, whether intentionally or due to circumstances beyond that parent's control, the court may order that a *lien* be placed on any real estate that he or she owns. A lien is a right that is given to the recipient to be paid out of the proceeds of any sale of the real estate. A lien can arise in two different ways, and different states may allow one or both types of liens.

The first is known as a *judgment lien*, and this type generally can be used in all states. The recipient must ask the court to order that the past-due support is a judgment, which then can be enforced the same as a judgment in any other lawsuit. Once the delinquency is reduced to a judgment, the recipient can file a lien with the county recorder's office in the county in which the real property is located. If the obligor tries to sell the property, the lien will show up on the title search that it held before the sale will go through. In order to convey clean title to the property, the obligor will have to satisfy the arrearage, by either paying off the amount due or having it taken out of the sale proceeds.

The second type of lien is a *statutory lien*. This lien arises automatically, typically after the past-due amount reaches a certain level or has been outstanding for a certain period. It is not necessary to have a court judgment for a statutory lien. Not all states provide for this type of lien. Check the law of your jurisdiction to see if statutory liens are allowed, and if so, what procedure needs to be followed to file the lien with the proper county's recorder of deeds office.

Visitation Interference

Typically, steps to enforce an order for visitation will be necessary in the case of interference by one of the parents, often the parent with custody. Visitation interference can take a number of forms. Sometimes, the custodial parent simply refuses to turn the children over to the other parent at the court-ordered time and place. However, the interference often is more insidious. Some tactics custodial parents use to keep the other parent from the children include:

- having the children enrolled in extracurricular activities during the scheduled time;
- claiming that the children are too ill to travel to the other parent's residence;
- bad-mouthing the other parent in front of the children; and,
- trying to change the children's last name from the name of the other parent, for example, by enrolling them in school under the custodial spouse's name.

In general, the legal remedies available for a noncustodial parent whose ex-spouse interferes with visitation can be either civil or criminal in nature. *Civil contempt penalties* are obtained by the wronged parent filing a motion for contempt asking the court to coerce the interfering parent into obeying the court's order. Possible remedies include an order for makeup visitation, an award of attorney's fees, or even jail time.

Criminal sanctions, if available, are provided by law of the jurisdiction in which the visitation order was entered. Some states treat visitation interference as a misdemeanor, while others consider it a felony. In some other jurisdictions, the severity of the crime increases if the interfering parent removes the child from the home state without the court's permission.

Interstate Enforcement

The two main statutes relating to child custody jurisdiction, the Uniform Child Custody Jurisdiction and Enforcement Act (UCCJEA) and the

Uniform Child Custody Jurisdiction Act (UCCJA), serve to clarify which court has jurisdiction over a particular child custody matter. (See Chapter 4 for more information.) As a result, a noncustodial parent is unable to remove a child from his or her home state and request a conflicting custody order in another jurisdiction. In any case where a petitioner comes into court to obtain an initial custody order, he or she must file an affidavit stating that there are no competing orders from other states already in effect.

As of the time of publication, almost every state either has adopted the UCCJEA to replace the UCCJA, or is in the process of doing so. Appendix B notes whether each particular state is a UCCJEA or a UCCJA state. In most states that have adopted the UCCJEA, the affidavit requirement remains the same as under the UCCJA. A sample **UCCJEA Affidavit** is included in Appendix C. (see form 7, p.247.) Please check the most recent laws in your state to be sure that you are proceeding under the correct statute.

Locating an Obligor Parent

The U.S. Department of Health and Human Services Office of Child Support Enforcement operates a program called the *Federal Parent Locator Service* (FPLS). The FPLS is a computerized database that allows certain authorized persons to access information on parents who are disobeying valid child support or child custody orders. The information is gathered from a variety of other governmental agencies: address and Social Security number information from the Social Security Administration, employment information from the Internal Revenue Service, and military service information from the Department of Defense, among others. The data then is used to track down child support deadbeats or noncustodial parents who may have fled the jurisdiction with their children in violation of standing child custody orders.

The FPLS encompasses a couple of other resources as well. The *National Directory of New Hires* (NDNH) is a database of employment information that the federal government requires each state to submit with regard to residents who obtain new employment within the state. The *Federal Case Registry* (FCR) is a catalog of child support cases from all states, with address and other information about the parties. With this network, the federal and various state child support enforcement offices have a powerful tool with which to locate noncustodial parents having child support arrearages, or even those who are guilty of parental kidnapping.

If you are the obligor with a child support arrearage hanging over your head, it is important to resolve the situation, or your divorce will go on and on in the form of post-dissolution collection proceedings. In the case where you truly have a change of circumstances causing an inability to pay at the court-ordered rate, the best way to proceed is to ask the court to modify the initial child support order. If the problem at the root of your failure to pay is temporary, you should at least pay something, even if it is not the full amount due. This may help establish to the court that you are acting in good faith, should the other parent seek to have you held in contempt.

CHAPTER 14:
Modification or Termination of Court Orders

With limited exceptions, a court can change or terminate maintenance, child support, and child custody orders after they have been entered, if the court decides that the change is necessary. A party who wants the change files a *petition for modification*. The standard the petitioner must meet is different depending on the type of order at stake.

Maintenance

An order for spousal support usually is subject to modification, either as to the amount or as to the duration. States sometimes treat different types of modifications in different ways. In some jurisdictions, maintenance is divided into two categories: maintenance ordered by the court, and maintenance agreed to by the parties. Maintenance that the court orders can be changed if a certain standard is met. Usually, the requirement is that there is a *substantial* or *material* change in circumstances.

In states that differentiate between court-ordered and agreed maintenance, alimony that is part of a contract between the parties usually can be modified only in whatever way the terms of the original agreement allow. Some states' courts have held that, in the case of a marital settlement agreement requiring modification to be in a writing and signed between the parties, the court will not change maintenance on the motion of only one of the parties.

The lesson to be learned from this is if you foresee wanting to change the spousal support terms of your marital settlement agreement at some point in the future, be sure to include in your agreement that modification may be by court order as well as by agreement.

Child Support

Typically, a court can modify the terms of a prior child support order by increasing or decreasing the amount or duration of the payments, as long as there is a *material change in circumstances* of one or both parties. A material change is one that will substantially affect the child's standard of living if the change is not allowed.

Some jurisdictions allow modification if there is a great enough discrepancy between the current amount of support ordered and what the state's statutory guidelines require. In such a case, a material change will be presumed. Illinois, for instance, permits a petition to modify in the case there is a 20% or greater inconsistency between the amount of support and the minimum required by state law.

Also, some states require that a certain amount of time pass before someone may go in and request a modification. Delaware, for example, will allow a motion to modify only after two and a half years have passed since the court entered the last support order. In general, only future support may be modified; past-due amounts may not be changed.

Change in Parental Income or Child's Need

Both parents are legally obligated to support their child. A change in the income of either parent, whether it be an increase or decrease in income, may be considered in ruling on a petition to modify support. Increased or decreased needs of the child also may be the basis for a petition. Examples of increased needs would include extraordinary health care expenses for a child's medical condition, and extra child care expenses related to a parent's employment or education.

Remarriage of Custodial Parent

Remarriage by the parent with primary custody of the child may or may not give a petitioner grounds for modification of support. Some states consider the economic condition and financial resources of the custodial parent's new spouse in determining whether to modify a support obligation, while other states do not. As a general rule, remarriage is not an automatic reason for modifying a support order. What counts is whether there is a change in the child's standard of living caused by the parent he or she lives with getting remarried that warrants a change in the allocation of the support obligation between the parents.

Obligation of Parent to New Family

When the parent who pays child support gets remarried and has children with the new spouse, some states allow this new obligation to be considered when deciding whether or not there will be a change in child support that has to be paid. Pennsylvania, for example, allows a proportional reduction (equal reduction in all outstanding child support orders) in child support if the payor's total child support obligation is more than 50% of his or her net monthly income.

Other states require that the children of the first marriage receive support according to the statutory guidelines before the later-born children are to be taken into account. In other words, first families come first, and second families come second.

Other Circumstances

Depending on the law of the particular state, other changes in circumstances also may support a child support modification. One example is when one of the parties begins to collect Social Security. The increase in income to the parent who has to pay child support may be enough to justify modifying child support upward. On the other hand, if it is the parent who receives the child support who has an increase in income because of Social Security, the child support might be decreased accordingly.

Another instance that might provide cause for a modification is when the child has his or her own income, such as a Social Security disability payment. Still another example is the case in which a child moves into the other parent's household. Obviously, it would not make sense for that parent to continue to pay child support to the other parent if the child has moved.

Termination of Child Support

Typically, state law provides that certain events trigger the termination of court-ordered child support payments. Most common among these events is the emancipation of the minor child. In most states, *emancipation* occurs upon the happening of one of the following events:

- the child reaches the age of majority, usually 18;
- the child marries;
- the child joins the military; or,
- the child is self-supporting and living on his or her own.

Another occurrence that ends the duty to pay child support would be if the minor child was adopted by another person. Of course, if the parties agreed to a termination date which the court approved, child support would also end at that date.

Child Custody

Child custody and visitation orders are modifiable, and state statutes set out the conditions that make modification acceptable. Most states require one or both of the following before a custody ruling may be changed:

- a change in circumstances that occurred since the current custody order was entered or
- it is in the best interest of the child that custody be modified.

Some jurisdictions ask only for a showing of the change in circumstances, while others are concerned only with the best interests of the child. Still others require a showing of both factors.

Change in Circumstances

The first element, change in circumstances, usually means that there has been some sort of a change in the child's living situation that affects the child's well-being. Some states' laws require a *substantial* or a *material* change. Some situations in which courts have found a change in circumstances include:

- frequent relocations by the custodial parent;
- psychological problems in the custodial parent;
- psychological problems in the child;
- domestic abuse by the custodial parent;
- substance abuse by the custodial parent;
- failure to obtain health care for the child;
- interference with the relationship between the noncustodial parent and the child by the custodial parent; and,
- difficulties in the relationship between the child and the new spouse of the custodial parent.

Physical disabilities generally are not by themselves a change; however, if the disabled parent is unable to care for the child, that may be the substantial change necessary to allow a modification. Other circumstances that do not qualify in and of themselves are remarriage or cohabitation by one of the parents, unless, as already discussed, the situation materially affects the child's welfare.

The evidence the petitioner must put forth in support of modification must be of a circumstance that occurred after the original custody order was entered. That is, evidence that was considered in making the initial determination of custody may not be presented again in asking for a custody change. In some jurisdictions, the petitioner must meet the burden of showing a change in circumstances before even getting to the question of what custody arrangement is in the best interest of the child.

Best Interests of the Child Standard

The *best interests of the child* standard is discussed in some detail in Chapter 11. For purposes of modifying a custody order, the standard is generally the same as it is for the initial custody determination. The court must find that, in light of all relevant factors put into evidence, a requested change of custody is what is best suited for the well-being of the child. Parents may not avoid going to the court to determine changes in child custody matters. The court holds the authority to decide what is in the best interests of the child, even if the parents have entered into an agreement about where the minor child will live.

As always, check the case law of your state to determine whether the circumstances of your particular case are likely to cause a court to change the existing custody arrangement.

Termination of Custody Orders

When a child is emancipated or no longer under the control of his or her parents, prior custody orders are no longer effective, and the court no longer has the authority to make custody decisions about the child.

Petitioning for Modification or Termination

Commencing an action to modify a prior custody order usually involves filing a petition to modify and an affidavit under either the UCCJA or the UCCJEA, depending on which law your state follows. These statutes have been covered in Chapter 13. Appendix C includes a sample **UCCJEA Affidavit,** which is similar to those used for UCCJA jurisdiction filings. (see form 7, p.247.)

In the event a custodial parent dies, states have very different policies as to the validity of the original custody order. In some states, the initial custody ruling becomes void immediately upon the death of the custodial parent, without any further court action by the other parent. In other states, the noncustodial parent must petition for a change in custody. Although courts generally find it appropriate to award custody to the noncustodial parent in such a case, this is not automatic.

You should note that a petition for modification may be an expensive and time-consuming proposition. If the petitioner alleges that the current arrangement is harming the child, the court may order physical and/or psychological examinations of some or all of the parties. It also may be a good idea to line up experts to testify in support of your case. The process, in fact, may be similar to the original custody hearing, with depositions and subpoenas. Many states also provide that attorneys' fees can be charged to the petitioner if the court finds that the petition was filed in order to harass the other parent. For that reason, you should examine your motivation for seeking the modification or termination. Be sure you are looking primarily to protect your child's best interest.

Afterword

A divorce can easily be among the most contentious legal matters a person will encounter in his or her lifetime. Divorce cases often are extremely stressful, not only because of the emotional toll taken on the parties, but also from the added upheaval that may result from the expense involved. If there are children involved, these cases may have the greatest effect on them. Following are several suggestions to decrease the negative impact of the divorce process, upon both you and your family.

First, find emotional support, for both yourself and your children. For you, this may mean close friends you can talk to or a trusted member of the clergy. Many areas have support groups for single parents or for those who are going through or trying to heal from a divorce. Having others to talk with who are going through the same things you are can be of great value to your emotional well-being.

There are support groups for children of divorce; check with local churches or your local courthouse. Professional counseling also can be very useful for both parents and children, although some may find therapy to be a costly alternative. Appendix A provides contact information that may help you to locate a qualified mental health professional; it is possible that some of them have a sliding scale for fees so that families with lower incomes would not have to pay the usual hourly rate.

Second, make sure that you are taking care of yourself physically. Some people have trouble eating during times of great stress; others may binge on unhealthy food. Some will find it difficult to keep a normal routine or may be unable to sleep. Unfortunately, some people initiate a self-destructive kind of pattern, such as drinking or drug use. Some who already have a substance abuse problem will sink more deeply into their addiction.

You should have your physician evaluate your physical condition periodically and attempt to keep a routine in which you allow yourself plenty of time to sleep. Watch what you eat, and take special care to avoid overindulging in alcohol. If you do not have a history of drug abuse, do not start. If drug use is a part of your life, continuing that pattern will only harm your case. If you are not able to stop on your own, seek professional help.

Third, keep your motives in the front of your mind as you proceed through your case. Be honest with yourself and, if you have children, remember that their well-being is the most important thing. Avoid doing things during the divorce process that are meant solely to harm the other parent. Also, do not place your children in the middle of the conflict by asking them to choose between you and their other parent. Do not put down your soon-to-be ex-spouse in front of your children. In most cases, your children love both you and their other parent, and hearing hurtful things about the other parent only hurts your children. Moreover, in time, they probably will figure out which parent, if any, has taken the high road and nurtured their relationship with the other parent. They may come to resent one parent when they realize that he or she tried to turn them against the other parent. At the very least, they will grow up to be very confused adults, and may even end up without the ability to work out interpersonal conflicts in a reasonable manner. Remember that, as a parent, you are the primary role model for your children.

Finally, regardless of the status of your divorce case or annulment, keep in mind that you might be able to revisit it later. Child support and maintenance can be reviewed if there is a change in circumstances of either party making it fair and equitable to change the support provisions. Child custody arrangements may be reviewed any time the best interests of the child requires it. For this reason, it is important to conduct yourself according to the court's wishes, even if you currently are not embroiled in litigation. In other words, if you are the one who has to pay spousal or child support, make sure you pay them in full and on time. If you are the parent who does not have custody of your children, make sure you use all of your visitation rights to see your children as much as you can.

Glossary

A

affiant. A person who executes and signs a written statement of testimony.

affidavit. Written testimony that is given under oath, signed, and notarized.

affinity. A relationship by marriage.

alimony (maintenance). Court-ordered financial support paid by one spouse to another, usually on a temporary basis.

annulment. A formal declaration that a marriage was invalid from the start (invalid ab initio).

answer. A document filed with the court in response to a petition or pleading filed by the other party in a case.

appeal. The formal process of asking a higher court to review and change a final order of a lower court.

B

bar association. An organization, whose membership is made up of attorneys practicing in a certain region, that exists for the professional support of its members.

best interests of the child. The standard according to which courts make custody, visitation, and support rulings, whereby the main consideration is what is of the greatest benefit to the child in question.

bilateral divorce. Proceeding for foreign dissolution of marriage in which both parties participate, even if one party appears not in person but through an attorney.

C

caption. The part of a pleading that sets out the names of the parties involved in a court case, as well as the case number.

case law. Judicial opinions handed down by judges who interpret the legislation.

case reporter. A volume of printed court decisions, often organized by state or region.

Child Support Recovery Act (CSRA). Federal statute making it a crime to willfully fail to make child support payments on behalf of a child living in another state.

collaborative divorce. A non-adversarial method of reaching a marital settlement agreement without resorting to court action, except to request the court to enter the divorce decree.

comity. A courtesy extended by one court to another court from another state or country, whereby the first court recognizes the orders of the foreign court.

community property. A method of dividing marital property, whereby assets acquired jointly by the spouses during the marriage are divided equally between the parties.

consanguinity. A blood relationship between persons.

contempt. A ruling that a party has willfully disobeyed an order of a court, with the possibility of civil or criminal penalties.

contingent fee. A payment arrangement for legal services, whereby the attorney retains a percentage of any cash settlement or award he or she has obtained on behalf of the client.

corroborating evidence. Additional, independent physical or testimonial evidence to support a fact asserted by a witness.

covenant marriage. A legal concept, enacted in several states, by which a couple seeking to marry agrees to receive premarital counseling and to waive the right to a no-fault divorce.

D

default. A court ruling that the responding party to a legal action has failed to make an appearance and therefore is prohibited from defending him- or herself in the action.

deposition. Out-of-court testimony, given under oath and transcribed by a court reporter in response to questions asked by the attorney for one of the parties to a legal action.

discovery. The process of gathering information from the other party to a legal action, using methods provided for by statute.

dissolution of marriage. A legal termination of marriage. Another term for *divorce*, used in many states.

divorce. *See dissolution of marriage.*

domicile. The home jurisdiction of a litigant, determined by actual physical presence in the jurisdiction without immediate intent to leave.

E

equitable distribution. A method of dividing marital property, used in a number of states, whereby the court takes into account a number of factors in determining a fair and equitable division of marital assets between the parties.

estoppel. The prohibition of challenging a legal procedure or outcome in court after accepting benefits from the procedure.

ex parte. A proceeding in which only one of the parties is present.

F

Federal Case Registry (FCR). A national database of state child support cases, with information on the parties, kept under the authority of the federal Office of Child Support Enforcement in order to locate delinquent child support obligors.

Federal Parent Locator Service (FPLS). A national network of information gathered from various federal agencies, used by state offices of child support enforcement to help locate child support deadbeats and noncustodial parents who have removed their children from the children's home state in violation of a valid custody order.

full faith and credit. Recognition by a state of the public policies and judicial processes of each of the other states, as required by the federal Constitution.

Full Faith and Credit for Child Support Orders Act (FFCCSOA). Federal statute requiring states to respect and enforce proper child support orders issued by the courts of other states.

G

grounds. The basis on which a petitioner is entitled to a dissolution of marriage.

guardian ad litem. A person appointed by the court in a custody case to represent the child's best interest.

I

interrogatories. A method of discovery whereby a number of written questions are served upon a party to a legal action to be answered in writing within a certain period of time; the subject matter of the interrogatories must be relevant to the legal action at hand.

J

joint custody. A court ruling where both parents are given shared physical and/or legal custody of a child.

jurisdiction. The authority of a court to hear a particular case.

L

legal custody. The right of a parent to make major life decisions on behalf of a minor child.

lien. A right that a creditor has to claim an interest in property owned by a debtor.

M

maintenance (alimony). Court-ordered financial support paid by one spouse to another, usually on a temporary basis.

manifest weight of the evidence. A standard against which a judgment is measured to determine if it is just; a ruling that is against the manifest weight of the evidence is clearly not supported by the evidence presented and may be overturned.

marital property. Assets belonging to both parties to a marriage, as opposed to separate property in which one spouse alone has an ownership interest.

mediation. A method of alternative dispute resolution where the parties meet with a neutral third party—often an attorney or social worker—to reach a mutually satisfactory resolution on various issues.

motion. A formal request for court action by a litigant, relating to the current legal proceedings, which the court will either grant or deny.

N

National Directory of New Hires (NDNH). A nationwide registry of employment information, part of the Federal Parent Locator Service, that is used to locate child support payors and enforce child support orders.

no-fault divorce. A legal concept whereby a party seeking to dissolve a marriage need not plead or prove a traditional ground for divorce; known in some states as *irreconcilable differences.*

non-wage garnishment. The confiscation and turnover of a debtor's personal property that is being held by a third party in order to satisfy the debt.

P

permanent maintenance. Spousal support that a court orders one spouse to pay to another spouse, with no fixed termination date unless a certain event occurs, such as the remarriage of the recipient spouse.

petition. A document filed with a court to initiate a formal legal action.

petitioner. The party who initiates a legal action by filing a formal pleading.

physical custody. The right of a parent to the actual residential possession of a minor child.

pleading. Generally, a document that sets forth assertions of fact and/or law, submitted to the court by a litigant in support of the litigant's claims.

pocket part. A paper pamphlet that fits into a built-in pocket in the back cover of certain legal books that provides an update to the law in the book.

prayer for relief. The section of a legal pleading in which a party makes a specific, detailed request for a ruling in his or her favor.

precedent. Prior case law relied upon to justify a legal decision in a later case with similar facts.

premarital agreement. A written agreement entered into by parties prior to their marriage, outlining terms of property settlement, spousal support and child custody in case of a dissolution of the marriage. Sometimes called a prenuptial agreement.

primary source. Legal research material comprised of original cases, statutes, and/or regulations, as promulgated by judges and legislatures, without additional commentary or explanation by a third party.

pro se. Representing oneself without the assistance of an attorney.

R

rehabilitative maintenance. Spousal support that the court orders one spouse to pay to another until such time as the recipient spouse has received suitable education or job training to make the spouse employable, so that maintenance no longer is needed.

respondent. A person who is served with notice that another party has initiated a legal action against the person.

retainer. A lump-sum advance payment to an attorney in order to secure the attorney's representation.

rule to show cause. A court order that directs a party to a lawsuit to appear before the court and explain why the party is failing to abide by a previous order of the court, with possible civil and criminal contempt penalties to follow in case the explanation is not forthcoming or is not legitimate.

S

secondary source. Legal research material that is derivative in nature, taking original legal source material such as court opinions and statutes and condensing, annotating, or explaining the material.

separate property. Assets belonging to one spouse alone, as opposed to marital property, which is owned jointly by both parties to a marriage.

service of process. The means by which a party is given notice of a legal proceeding affecting the rights of the party, generally by either delivering written notice of the proceeding to the party or to someone of appropriate age living in his or her household, or in some cases, by publishing notice in the newspaper.

sheriff's sale. The selling of confiscated personal property of a debtor by county law enforcement, the proceeds of which are used to satisfy the debt.

simplified divorce. A legal procedure whereby a divorce is granted on a summary, condensed basis, if the parties meet certain requirements, such as having been separated for a certain period of time before filing the dissolution action.

T

temporary maintenance. Spousal support that the court orders one spouse to pay to the other during the pendency of the divorce proceedings.

U

uncontested divorce. A dissolution of marriage that is granted 1) after the respondent to a petition for dissolution has failed to file a response to the petition or to appear before the court, or 2) because the parties have agreed to all terms of the dissolution and the parties have agreed that no appearance is necessary.

Uniform Child Custody Jurisdiction Act (UCCJA). Uniform statute still in force in several states, but replaced by the UCCJEA in most others, to create consistent laws throughout the United States in order to prevent parental kidnapping and removal of children across state lines.

Uniform Child Custody Jurisdiction and Enforcement Act (UCCJEA). Uniform statute enacted by most of the states, to create consistent laws throughout the United States in order to prevent parental kidnapping and removal of children across state lines.

Uniform Interstate Family Support Act (UIFSA). Statute enacted in all states that governs, among other things, which state has continuing and exclusive jurisdiction over child support issues in a particular case.

V

venue. The appropriate court in which to bring a legal action; a dissolution action typically must be commenced in a trial court in the county in which one of the parties (sometimes the petitioner, sometimes the respondent, and sometimes either one) resides.

verification. A sworn statement at the end of a legal document, subjecting the declarant to penalties of perjury, that the matters contained in the document are true.

W

wage deduction. Court-ordered withholding of a certain amount of money from each of a delinquent obligor's paychecks until past-due amounts are satisfied.

APPENDIX A:
Resources

Lawyer Referral Services by State

ALABAMA
Birmingham Bar Lawyer Referral Service
Birmingham, AL
205-251-8006
www.birminghambar.org

Madison County Lawyer Referral and Information Service
Huntsville, AL
205-539-2275

Mobile Bar Association Lawyer Referral Service
Mobile, AL
251-433-1032
www.mobilebar.com

Alabama State Bar
Lawyer Referral Service
Montgomery, AL
800-392-5660
www.alabar.org/lrs

ALASKA
Alaska Bar Association Lawyer Referral Service
Anchorage, AK
907-272-0352
800-770-9999 (in-state)
www.alaskabar.org

ARIZONA
Maricopa County Lawyer Referral Service
Phoenix, AZ
602-257-4434
www.maricopabar.org

Pima County Bar Association Lawyer Referral Service
Tucson, AZ
520-623-4625

State Bar of Arizona Find a Lawyer
www.azbar.org/LegalResources/findlawyer.cfm

ARKANSAS
Arkansas Bar Association
www.Arkansasfindalawyer.com

CALIFORNIA
Attorney Search Network
www.california-lawyer-referral.org/getalawyer.ctm
877-437-3337

The State Bar of California
Lawyer Referral Services Program
San Francisco, CA
www.calbar.ca.gov
866-442-2529 (in state)
415-538-2250 (out of state)

Attorney Referral and Information Service of the Fresno County Bar
Association
Fresno, CA
559-264-0137
www.fresnocountybar.org

Contra Costa County Bar Association Lawyer Referral and Information
Service
Martinez, CA
925-825-5700
www.cccba.org

East San Diego County Lawyer Referral Service
El Cajon, CA
619-588-1936

Lawyer Referral Service Humboldt County Bar Association
Eureka, CA
707-445-0866

Lawyer Referral Service of Bar Association of Northern San Diego County
Vista, CA
760-758-4755
www.bansdc.org

Lawyer Referral Service of Santa Barbara County
Carpenteria, CA 93014
805-569-9400
www.sblaw.org

Lawyer Referral Service of Santa Cruz County
Santa Cruz, CA
831-425-4755
www.santacruzbar.org

Lawyer Referral Service of the Marin County Bar Association
San Rafael, CA
415-499-1813
www.marinbar.org

Lawyer Referral Service of the Riverside County Bar Association
Riverside, CA
951-682-7520
www.riversidecountybar.com

Lawyer Referral Service of the San Joaquin County Bar Association
Stockton, CA
209-948-4620
www.sjcbar.org

Lawyer Referral Service of the San Mateo County Bar Association
Redwood City, CA
650-369-4149
www.smcba.org

Lawyer Referral Service of the Solano County Bar Association
Fairfield, CA
707-422-0127
www.solanobar.org

Lawyer Referral Service of the South Bay Bar Association
Chula Vista, CA
619-422-5377
www.southbaybarassociation.com

Lawyers Referral Service of the Stanislaus County Bar Association
Modesto, CA
209-571-5727
www.stanbar.org

Los Angeles County Bar Association Lawyer Referral and Information Service
Los Angeles, CA
213-243-1525
www.smartlaw.org

Merced County Bar Lawyer Referral Service
Merced, CA
209-383-3886

Monterey County Bar Association Lawyer Referral Service
Salinas, CA
831-663-6955
www.montereycountybar.org

Nevada County Lawyer Referral Service
Grass Valley, CA
530-272-5962
www.nevadacountybar.com

Orange County Bar Association Lawyer Referral and Information Service
Irvine, CA
949-440-6747
www.ocbar.org

San Bernardino County Bar Association Lawyer Referral Service
San Bernardino, CA
909-888-6791
www.SBCBA.org

San Luis Obispo County Bar Association Lawyer Referral and Information Service
San Luis Obispo, CA
805-788-2099
www.slobar.org

Santa Clara County Bar Association Lawyer Referral Service
San Jose, CA
408-287-2557
408-971-6822 (for modest means or workman's comp)
www.sccba.com

Sonoma County Lawyer Referral Service
Sonoma, CA
707-546-5297
www.sonomacountybar.org

Tulare County Bar Association Lawyer Referral Service
Visalia, CA
559-732-2513

Ventura County Bar Association Lawyer Referral Service
Ventura, CA
805-650-7599
www.vcba.org

COLORADO
El Paso County Bar Association Lawyer Referral Service
Colorado Springs, CO
719-473-9700
www.elpasocountybar.org

Metropolitan Lawyer Referral Service
Denver, CO
303-831-8000 (Denver and Boulder)
970-226-2455 (Ft. Collins)
www.mlrsonline.org

CONNECTICUT
Fairfield County Lawyer Referral Service
Fairfield, CT
203-335-4116

Hartford County Bar Association Lawyer Referral Service
Hartford, CT
860-525-6052

New Haven County Bar Association Lawyer Referral Service
New Haven, CT
203-562-5750
www.newhavenbar.org

New London County Bar Association Lawyer Referral Service
Yantic, CT
860-889-9384

DISTRICT OF COLUMBIA
Bar Association of the District of Columbia Lawyer Referral Service
Washington, D.C.
202-296-7845
www.badc.org

DELAWARE
Delaware State Bar Association Lawyer Referral Service
Wilmington, DE
302-478-8850
800-773-0606 (in state)
www.dsba.org

FLORIDA
Clearwater Bar Association Lawyer Referral Service
Clearwater, FL
727-461-4880
www.clearwaterbar.org

Broward County Bar Association Lawyer Referral Service
Fort Lauderdale, FL
954-764-8310
www.browardbar.org

Lee County Bar Association Lawyer Referral Service
Fort Myers, FL
239-334-4491
www.leebar.org

Jacksonville Bar Association
Jacksonville, FL
904-399-5780
www.jaxbar.org

Collier County Bar Association Lawyer Referral Service
Naples, FL
239-774-8138
www.colliercountybar.org

Orange County Bar Association
Orlando, FL
407-422-4537
www.orangecountybar.org

Escambia/Santa Rosa Bar Association Lawyer Referral Service
Pensacola, FL
850-434-6009
www.esrba.com

Saint Petersburg Bar Association Lawyer Referral Service
Saint Petersburg, FL
727-821-5450
www.stpetebar.com

Florida Bar Lawyer Referral Service
Tallahassee, FL
800-342-8011
www.flabar.org

Tallahassee Bar Association
Tallahassee, FL
850-681-0601
www.tallahasseebar.org

Hillsborough County Bar Association Lawyer Referral Service
Tampa, FL
813-221-7780
www.hillsbar.com

Palm Beach County Bar Association Lawyer Referral and Information Service
West Palm Beach, FL
561-687-3266
561-451-3256 (Boca/Delray)
www.palmbeachbar.org

GEORGIA
Atlanta Bar Lawyer Referral Service
Atlanta, GA
404-521-0777
www.atlantabar.org

DeKalb Bar Association
Decatur, GA
404-373-2580
www.dekalbbar.org

Cobb County Lawyer Referral Service
Marietta, GA
770-424-7149
www.cobbar.org

Savannah Bar Association Lawyer Referral Service
Savannah, GA
912-651-2752

HAWAII
Hawaii State Bar Association Lawyer Referral and Information Service
Honolulu, HI
808-537-9140
www.hawaiilawyerreferral.com

IDAHO
Idaho State Bar Lawyer Referral Service
Boise, ID
208-334-4500
www2.state.id.us/ISB

ILLINOIS
Northwest Suburban Bar Association Attorney Referral Service
Palatine, IL
847-259-7908
www.nwsba.org

Chicago Bar Association Lawyer Referral Service
Chicago, IL
312-554-2071
www.chicagobar.org

DuPage County Bar Association Lawyer Referral Service
Wheaton, IL
630-653-9109
www.dcba.org

West Suburban Bar Association Lawyer Referral Service
Forest Park, IL
708-366-1122

Kane County Bar Association Lawyer Referral Service
Geneva, IL
630-762-1900
www.kanecountybar.org

North Suburban Bar Association Lawyer Referral Service
Glenview, IL
847-564-4800
www.ilnsba.org

Will County Bar Association
Joliet, IL
815-726-0383
815-726-1015
www.willcountybar.com

Peoria County Lawyer Referral Service
Peoria, IL
309-674-1224
www.peoriabar.org

South Suburban Bar Association Lawyer Referral Service
Oak Forest, IL
708-633-9700

Winnebago County Lawyer Referral Service
Rockford, IL
815-964-5152
www.wcbarockford.org

Lake County Bar Association Lawyer Referral Service
Waukegan, IL
847-244-3140
www.lakebar.org

Illinois State Bar Association
217-525-5297
800-922-8757
IllinoisLawyerFinder.com

INDIANA
Lake County Bar Association
Crown Point, IN
219-738-1905
www.lakecountybar.com

Evansville Bar Association Lawyer Referral Service
Evansville, IN
812-426-1712
www.evvbar.org

Allen County Bar Association Lawyer Referral Service
Fort Wayne, IN
260-423-2358
www.allencountybar.org

Indianapolis Bar Association Lawyer Referral Service
Indianapolis, IN
317-269-2222
www.indybar.org

Saint Joseph County Bar Association Lawyer Referral Service
South Bend, IN
574-235-9657
www.sjcba.org

IOWA
Iowa State Bar Association Lawyer Referral Service
Des Moines, IA
800-532-1108 (in state)
515-280-7429
www.iowabar.org

KANSAS
Kansas Bar Association
Topeka, KS
800-928-3111
www.ksbar.org

Wichita Bar Association Lawyer Referral Service
Wichita, KS
316-263-2251
www.wichitabar.org

KENTUCKY
Northern Kentucky Bar Association
Crestview Hills, KY
859-781-1300
www.nkybar.com

Central Kentucky Lawyer Referral Service
Lexington, KY
859-225-8644
www.centralkylawyers.com

Attorney Referral Service (Boyd, Greenup, and Lewis Counties)
Ashland, KY
606-326-1313

Kentucky Lawyer Referral Service
Louisville, KY
502-583-1801
www.loubar.org

LOUISIANA
Baton Rouge Bar Association Lawyer Referral and Information Service
Baton Rouge, LA
225-344-9926
www.brba.org

Southwest Louisiana Lawyer Referral Service
Lake Charles, LA
337-436-2914
337-497-0090

New Orleans Bar Association Lawyer Referral Service
New Orleans, LA
504-561-8828
www.neworleansbar.org

Shreveport Lawyer Referral Service
Shreveport, LA
318-222-3643
www.shreveportbar.com

MAINE
Maine State Bar Association Lawyer Referral and Information Service
Augusta, ME
800-860-1460
www.mainebar.org

MARYLAND
Anne Arundel Bar Association Lawyer Referral Service
Annapolis, MD
410-280-6950
410-280-6961
www.aabar.org

Baltimore City Bar Association
Baltimore, MD
410-539-3112
www.baltimorebar.org

Howard County Bar Association Lawyer Referral Service
Ellicott City, MD
410-313-2030
www.howardcountybar.org

Bar Association of Montgomery County Lawyer Referral Service
Rockville, MD
301-279-9100
www.montbar.org

Baltimore County Lawyer Referral Service
Towson, MD
410-337-9100
www.bcba.org

Prince George's County Bar Association Lawyer Referral Service
Upper Marlboro, MD
301-952-1440
866-757-7785
www.pgcba.com

Carroll County Lawyer Referral and Information Service
Westminster, MD
410-876-6565

Frederick County Lawyer Referral and Information Service
Frederick, MD
301-663-1139

MASSACHUSETTS
Massachusetts Bar Association Lawyer Referral and Information Service
Boston, MA
866-627-7577 (in state)
617-654-0400
www.massbar.org

Boston Bar Association Lawyer Referral Service
Boston, MA
617-742-0625
www.bostonbar.org

Middlesex County Bar Association Lawyer Referral Service
Cambridge, MA
617-494-4150

Bristol County Bar Association Lawyer Referral Service
New Bedford, MA
508-990-1303

Hampshire County Bar Association Lawyer Referral Service
Northampton, MA
413-586-8729

Essex County Bar Association Lawyer Referral Service
Salem, MA
978-741-7888
800-228-2574
www.essexcountybar.org

Hampden County Bar Association Lawyer Referral Service
Springfield, MA
413-732-4648

Worcester County Bar Association Lawyer Referral Service
Worcester, MA
508-752-1311
800-622-9700
www.worcestercountybar.org

MICHIGAN

Washtenaw County Bar Association Lawyer Referral and Information Service
Ann Arbor, MI
734-996-3229
www.washbar.org

Oakland County Lawyer Referral Service
Bloomfield Hills, MI
248-338-2100
www.ocba.org

Detroit Metropolitan Bar Association Lawyer Referral Service
Detroit, MI
313-961-3545
www.detroitlawyer.org

Genesee County Bar Association Lawyer Referral Service
Flint, MI
810-232-6000
www.gcbalaw.org

Grand Traverse Leelenau Antrim Attorney Referral Service
Traverse City, MI
231-922-4715
www.gtlabar.org

Ingham County Bar Association Lawyer Referral and Information Service
Lansing, MI
517-482-8816

State Bar of Michigan Lawyer Referral Service
Lansing, MI
800-968-0738
517-346-6300
www.michbar.org

Macomb County Bar Association
Mt. Clemens, MI
586-468-2940
www.macombbar.org

MINNESOTA
Hennepin County Bar Association Lawyer Referral and Information Service
Minneapolis, MN
612-752-6666
www.hcba.org

Minnesota State Bar Association
Minneapolis, MN
612-333-1183
800-292-4152 (in state)
www.mnbar.org

Ramsey County Bar Association Attorney Referral Service
Saint Paul, MN
651-224-1775
www.ramseybar.org

MISSISSIPPI
Mississippi Bar Association
Jackson, MS 39225
601-948-4471 (Directory service—not a lawyer referral service)
www.msbar.org

Hinds County Bar Association
Jackson, MS 39201
601-969-6097

MISSOURI
Missouri Bar Association Lawyer Referral Service
Jefferson City, MO
573-636-3635
www.mobar.org

Kansas City Metropolitan Bar Association Lawyer Referral Service
Kansas City, MO
816-221-9472
www.kcmba.org

Springfield Metropolitan Bar Association
Springfield, MO
417-831-2783
www.smba.cc

St Louis Metropolitan Bar Association Lawyer Referral Service
St. Louis, MO
314-621-6681
www.bamsl.org

MONTANA
Montana Lawyer Referral Service
Helena, MT
406-449-6577
www.montanabar.org

NEBRASKA
Nebraska State Bar Association Lawyer Referral Service
Lincoln, NE
402-475-7091
800-927-0117 (in state)
www.nebar.com

Omaha Bar Association Lawyer Referral Service
Omaha, NE
402-280-3603
www.omahabarassociation.com

NEVADA
Nevada State Bar Lawyer Referral and Information Service
Las Vegas, NV
702-382-0504
800-789-5747 (in state)
www.nvbar.org

NEW HAMPSHIRE
New Hampshire Bar Association Lawyer Referral Service
Concord, NH
603-229-0002
www.nhbar.org

NEW JERSEY
Atlantic County Bar Association Lawyer Referral Service
Atlantic City, NJ
609-345-3444

Camden County Bar Association Lawyer Referral Service
Cherry Hill, NJ
856-964-4520

Cape May County Bar Association Lawyer Referral Service
Cape May, NJ
856-482-0620

Union County Lawyer Referral Service
Elizabeth, NJ
908-354-5984
www.uclaw.com

Monmouth Bar Association Lawyer Referral Service
Freehold,NJ
732-431-5544

Bergen County Bar Association Lawyer Referral Service
Hackensack, NJ
201-488-0032
www.bergenbar.org

Mercer County Bar Association Lawyer Referral Service
Hamilton, NJ
609-585-6200
www.mercerbar.com

Morris County Bar Association Lawyer Referral Service
Sussex County Lawyer Referral Service
Morristown, NJ
973-267-5882
www.morriscountybar.com

Warren County Lawyer Referral Service
Belvidere, NJ
908-387-1835

Burlington County Bar Association Lawyer Referral Service
Mount Holly, NJ
609-261-4862
www.burlcobar.org

Middlesex County Bar Association Lawyer Referral Service
New Brunswick, NJ
732-828-0053
www.mcbalaw.com

Essex County Bar Association Lawyer Referral Service
Livingston, NJ
973-533-6775
www.essexbar.com

Passaic County Bar Association Lawyer Referral Service
Paterson, NJ
973-345-4585
www.passaicbar.org

Hunterdon County Bar Association Lawyer Referral Service
Annandale, NJ
908-735-2611

Somerset County Bar Association Lawyer Referral Service
Somerville, NJ
908-685-2323

Cumberland County Bar Association Lawyer Referral Service
Vineland, NJ
856-692-0960
www.cumbnjbarassoc.org

Gloucester County Lawyer Referral Service
Woodbury, NJ
856-848-4071
www.gcbanj.org

NEW MEXICO
Albuquerque Bar Association Lawyer Referral Service
Albuquerque, NM
505-243-2615
www.abqbar.com

State Bar Association of New Mexico
Albuquerque, NM
505-797-6066
800-876-6227
www.nmbar.org

NEW YORK
New York State Bar Association Lawyer Referral and Information Service
Albany, NY
800-342-3661
518-487-5709
www.nysba.org

Albany County Bar Association Lawyer Referral Service
Albany, NY
518-445-7691
www.albanycountybar.com

Bronx County Bar Association Lawyer Referral Service
Bronx, NY
718-293-5600
www.bronxbar.com

Broome County Bar Association Lawyer Referral Service
Binghamton, NY
607-723-6331
www.bcbar.org

Chemung County Lawyer Referral Service
Elmira, NY
607-734-9687
800-348-0448

Cattaraugus County Bar Association Lawyer Referral and Information Service
Gowanda, NY
716-532-3351

Dutchess County Bar Association Lawyer Referral Service
Poughkeepsie, NY
845-473-2488

Erie County Bar Association Lawyer Referral and Information Service
Buffalo, NY
716-852-3100
www.eriebar.org

Brooklyn Bar Association Lawyer Referral Service
Brooklyn, NY
718-624-0675
www.brooklynbar.org

Monroe County Bar Association Lawyer Referral and Information Service
Rochester, NY
585-546-2130
www.mcba.org

Nassau County Bar Association Lawyer Referral and Information Service
Mineola, NY
516-747-4070
www.nassaubar.org

Association of the Bar of the City of New York Lawyer Referral Service
New York, NY
212-626-7373
www.nycbar.org

Onondaga County Bar Association Lawyer Referral Service
Syracuse, NY
315-471-2690
www.onbar.org

Orange County Bar Association Lawyer Referral Service
Goshen, NY
845-294-8222
www.orangelaw.org

Putnam County Bar Association Lawyer Referral Service
Carmel, NY
845-225-4904

Queens County Bar Association Lawyer Referral Service
Jamaica, NY
718-291-4500
www.qcba.org

Rensselaer County Bar Association Lawyer Referral Service
Troy, NY
518-272-7220

Richmond County Bar Association Lawyer Referral Service
Staten Island, NY
718-442-4500
www.richmondcountybar.org

Rockland County Bar Association Lawyer Referral Service
New City, NY
845-634-2149
www.rocklandbar.org

Suffolk County Bar Association Lawyer Referral and Information Service
Hauppage, NY
631-234-5577
www.scba.org

Sullivan County Bar Association
Monticello, NY
845-794-2426

Warren County Bar Association Lawyer Referral Service
Glens Falls, NY
518-792-9239
www.wcba-ny.com

Westchester County Bar Association Lawyer Referral Service
White Plains, NY
914-761-5151
www.wcbany.org

NORTH CAROLINA
North Carolina Lawyer Referral Service
Cary, NC
919-677-8574
800-662-7660 (in-state)
www.ncbar.org

Mecklenburg County Bar Association Lawyer Referral Service
Charlotte, NC
704-375-8624
www.meckbar.org

NORTH DAKOTA
State Bar Association of North Dakota Lawyer Referral Service
Bismarck, ND
701-255-1404
800-472-2685 (in state)

OHIO
Akron Bar Association Lawyer Referral and Information Service
Akron, OH
330-253-5038
www.akronbar.org

Clermont County Bar Association Lawyer Referral Service
Batavia, OH
513-732-7109
www.clermontlawlibrary.com

Stark County Lawyer Referral Service
Canton, OH
330-453-0686
www.starkctybar.com

Cincinnati Bar Association Lawyer Referral Service
Cincinnati, OH
513-381-8359
www.cincybar.org

Cuyahoga County Bar Association Lawyer Referral Service
Cleveland, OH
216-621-2414
www.cuybar.org

Cleveland Bar Association Lawyer Referral Service
Cleveland, OH
216-696-3532
877-CLEV-BAR
www.clevelandbar.org

Columbus Bar Association Lawyer Referral Service
Columbus, OH
614-221-0754
877-560-1014
www.cbalaw.org

Dayton Bar Association Lawyer Referral Service
Dayton, OH
937-222-6102
www.daybar.org

Butler County Bar Association Lawyer Referral Service
Hamilton, OH
513-896-6671
www.butlercountybar.org

Hocking County Bar Association
Logan, OH
740-385-5604
Medina County Bar Association Lawyer Referral Service
Medina, OH
330-725-9794
www.medinabar.org

Lake County Bar Association Lawyer Referral Service
Painesville, OH
440-352-6044
www.lcba-ohio.org

Toledo Bar Association Lawyer Referral Service
Toledo, OH
419-242-2000
www.toledobar.org

Mahoning County Bar Lawyer Referral Service
Youngstown, OH
330-746-2933
330-746-2737
www.mahoningbar.org

OKLAHOMA
Tulsa County Bar Association Lawyer Referral Service
Tulsa, OK
918-584-5243
www.tulsabar.com

OREGON
Oregon State Bar Lawyer Referral Service
Lake Oswego, OR
503-684-3763
800-452-8260 (in state)
www.osbar.org

PENNSYLVANIA
Lehigh County Bar Association Lawyer Referral Service
Allentown, PA
610-433-7094
www.lehighbar.org

Cumberland County Bar Association Lawyer Referral Service
Carlisle, PA
717-249-3166
800-990-9108 (in state)
www.ccba.pa.net

Bucks County Bar Association Lawyer Referral Service
Doylestown, PA
215-348-9413
888-991-9922
www.bucksbar.org

Northampton County Bar Association
Easton, PA
610-258-6333
www.norcobar.org

Erie County Bar Association Lawyer Referral Service
Erie, PA
814-459-4411
www.eriebar.com

Westmoreland County Bar Association Lawyer Referral Service
Greensburg, PA
724-834-8490
www.westbar.org

Dauphin County Bar Association Lawyer Referral Service
Harrisburg, PA
717-232-7536
www.dcba-pa.org

Pennsylvania Bar Association Lawyer Referral Service
Harrisburg, PA
717-238-6807
800-692-7375 (in state)
www.pabar.org

Lancaster Bar Association Lawyer Referral Service
Lancaster, PA
717-393-0737
www.lancasterbar.org

Delaware County Bar Association Lawyer Referral Service
Media, PA
610-566-6625
www.barristersclub.com
www.delcobar.org

Montgomery County Lawyer Referral Service
Norristown, PA
610-279-9660
800-560-5219
www.montgomerybar.org

Blair County Bar Association Lawyer Referral Service
Hollidaysburg, PA
814-693-3090

Philadelphia Bar Association Lawyer Referral and Information Service
Philadelphia, PA
215-238-6300
www.philabar.org

Beaver County Bar Association Lawyer Referral Service
Beaver, PA
724-728-4888
www.bcba-pa.org

Lackawanna County Bar Association Lawyer Referral Service
Scranton, PA
570-969-9161
www.lackawannabar.com

Mercer County Bar Association Lawyer Referral Service
Mercer, PA
724-342-3111

Monroe County Bar Association Lawyer Referral Service
Stroudsburg, PA
570-424-7288
www.monroebar.org

Allegheny County Bar Association Lawyer Referral Service
Pittsburgh, PA
412-261-6161
www.acba.org

Berks County Lawyer Referral Service
Reading, PA
610-375-4591
www.berksbar.com

Washington County Bar Association Lawyer Referral Service
Washington, PA
724-225-6710
www.washcobar.org

Chester County Bar Association Lawyer Referral Service
West Chester, PA
610-429-1500
www.chescobar.org

Luzerne County Lawyer Referral Service
Wilkes-Barre, PA
570-822-6029
www.wblawlibrary.org

York County Lawyer Referral Service
York, PA
717-854-8755
www.yorkbar.com

RHODE ISLAND
Rhode Island Bar Association Lawyer Referral Service
Providence, RI
401-421-7799
www.ribar.com

SOUTH CAROLINA
South Carolina Bar Association Lawyer Referral Service
Columbia, SC
800-868-2284
803-799-7100
www.scbar.org

SOUTH DAKOTA
South Dakota State Bar Lawyer Referral Service
Pierre, SD
605-224-7554
800-952-2333 (in state)
www.sdbar.org

TENNESSEE
Knoxville Bar Association Lawyer Referral Service
Knoxville, TN
865-522-7501
www.knoxbar.org

Chattanooga Bar Association Lawyer Referral Service
Chattanooga, TN
423-266-5950
www.chattbar.org

Tennessee Bar Association Southeast Tennessee Lawyer Referral Service
Nashville, TN
423-756-3222
www.tba.org

Nashville Bar Association Lawyer Referral Service
Nashville, TN
615-242-6546 (middle and west Tennessee)
865-522-7501 (east Tennessee)
423-756-3222 (southeast Tennessee)
www.nashbar.org

TEXAS

State Bar of Texas Lawyer Referral and Information Service
Austin, TX
800-252-9690
512-463-1463
www.texasbar.com

Jefferson County Bar Association Lawyer Referral Service
Beaumont, TX
409-835-8438
www.jcba.org

Corpus Christi Bar Association Lawyer Referral Service
Corpus Christi, TX
361-883-3971
www.ccbar.com

Dallas Bar Association Lawyer Referral Service
Dallas, TX
214-220-7444
www.dallasbar.org

El Paso Bar Association Lawyer Referral Service
El Paso, TX
915-532-7052
www.elpasobar.com

Tarrant County Bar Association Lawyer Referral Service
Fort Worth, TX
817-336-4101
www.tarrantbar.org

Houston Lawyer Referral Service, Inc.
Houston, TX
713-237-9429
800-289-4577
www.hlrs.org

San Antonio Bar Association Lawyer Referral Service
San Antonio, TX
210-227-8822
www.sanantoniobar.org

UTAH
Utah Bar Association LegalMatch
866-678-5342
http://utahbar.legalmatch.com

VERMONT
Vermont Bar Association Lawyer Referral Service
Montpelier, VT
802-223-2020
800-639-7036
www.vtbar.org

VIRGINIA
Alexandria Lawyer Referral Service
Alexandria, VA
703-548-1105
www.alexandriabarassoc.com

Arlington County Bar Association Lawyer Referral Service
Arlington, VA
703-228-3390
http://patriot.net/~crouch/lrs.html

Fairfax Bar Association Lawyer Referral Service
Fairfax, VA
703-246-3780
www.fairfaxbar.org

Lawyer Referral Service of the Norfolk & Portsmouth Bar Association
Norfolk, VA
757-623-0132
www.norfolkandportsmouthbar.org

Charlottesville-Albemarle Legal Aid Society Lawyer Referral Service
Charlottesville, VA
434-977-0553
800-578-8111
www.cabaonline.org

Virginia Lawyer Referral Service
Richmond, VA
804-775-0808
800-552-7977
www.vsb.org

WASHINGTON
Kitsap County Lawyer Referral Service
Bremerton, WA
360-373-2426
www.kitsaplegalservices.org

Lewis County Lawyer Referral Program
Chehalis, WA
360-748-0430
www.wsba.org

Snohomish County Bar Association Referral Service
Everett, WA
425-388-3056
www.snobar.org

King County Bar Lawyer Referral Service
Seattle, WA
206-267-7010
www.kcba.org

Tacoma-Pierce County Bar Association Lawyer Referral
Tacoma, WA
253-383-3432
www.tpcba.com

Southwest Washington Lawyer Referral Service
Vancouver, WA
360-695-0599

WEST VIRGINIA
West Virginia State Bar Lawyer Referral Service
Charleston, WV
304-558-7991
www.wvbar.org

WISCONSIN
Wisconsin State Bar Lawyer Referral and Information Service
Madison, WI
800-362-9082 (in state)
608-257-4666
www.legalexplorer.com

Milwaukee Bar Association Lawyer Referral and Information Service
Milwaukee, WI
414-274-6768
www.milwbar.org

WYOMING
Wyoming State Bar Association Lawyer Referral Service
Cheyenne, WY
307-632-9061
www.wyomingbar.org

Statutory References

Legal Information Institute
www.law.cornell.edu

American Bar Association
321 North Clark Street
Chicago, IL 60610
800-285-2221
www.abanet.org

Overseas Divorce

United States Department of State
888-407-4747
www.travel.state.gov/law

Mediation

Association of Family and Conciliation Courts
6525 Grand Teton Plaza
Madison, WI 53719
608-664-3750
www.afccnet.org

Association for Conflict Resolution
1015 18th Street, NW
Suite 1150
Washington, DC 20036
202-464-9700
www.acrnet.org

Collaborative Divorce

International Academy of Collaborative Professionals
145 Wildhorse Valley Road
Novato, CA 94947
415-897-2398
www.collaborativepractice.com

Tax Considerations

United States Internal Revenue Service
www.irs.gov

Child Custody

American Psychological Association
750 First Street, NE
Washington, DC 20002
202-336-5500
800-374-2721
www.apa.org

American Psychiatric Association
1000 Wilson Boulevard
Suite 1825
Arlington, VA 22209
703-907-7300
www.psych.org/edu

Child Support Enforcement

Office of Child Support Enforcement
Administration for Children and Families
370 L'Enfant Promenade, SW
Washington, DC 20447
202-401-9373
www.acf.hhs.gov

Association for Children for Enforcement of Support
P.O. Box 7842
Fredericksburg, VA 22404
888-310-2237
www.childsupport-aces.org

Domestic Violence

U.S. Department of Justice
Office on Violence Against Women
950 Pennsylvania Avenue, NW
Washington, DC 20530
202-514-2000
www.usdoj.gov/ovw

Family Violence Prevention Fund
383 Rhode Island Street
Suite #304
San Francisco, CA 94103
415-252-8900
www.endabuse.org

Parental Kidnapping

National Center for Missing & Exploited Children
699 Prince Street
Alexandria, VA 22314
800-843-5678
www.missingkids.com

Department of State
Office of Children's Issues
2201 C Street, NW
CA/OCS/CI
Washington, DC 20520
202-736-9090
http://travel.state.gov/family/family_1732

General

Findlaw
www.findlaw.com

Legal Information Institute
www.law.cornell.edu

APPENDIX B:
State-by-State Laws

Alabama

Statute

Code of Alabama beginning with Section 30-2-1.

Venue

Complaint for divorce to be filed: (1) in the circuit court of the county in which the defendant resides, or (2) in the circuit court of the county in which the parties resided when the separation occurred, or (3) if the defendant is a nonresident, in the circuit court of the county in which the other party to the marriage resides. (Sec. 30-2-4.)

Grounds

(1) Physical and incurable incapacitation at the time of the marriage; (2) adultery; (3) voluntary abandonment from bed and board for one year preceding the filing of the complaint; (4) imprisonment in the penitentiary of any state for two years, with a sentence of seven years or longer; (5) commission of the crime against nature, either before or after the marriage; (6) habitual drunkenness or drug use; (7) "complete incompatibility of temperament" that the parties can no longer live together; (8) confinement in a mental hospital for five years due to incurable insanity;

(9) irretrievable breakdown of the marriage such that further attempts at reconciliation are impractical or futile and not in the best interests of the parties or family [no-fault divorce]; (10) pregnancy of wife by another man at the time of marriage, without husband's knowledge; (11) commission of violence or reasonable apprehension of such violence; (12) the parties have lived separate and apart for two years preceding the filing of the complaint. (Sec. 30-2-1.)

Residency
When the defendant is a nonresident, the plaintiff must have been a bona fide resident for six months before the filing of the complaint; if both are residents, there is no time requirement. (Sec. 30-2-5.)

Property Division
Equitable distribution. (beginning with Sec. 30-4-1.)

Maintenance
Fault may be considered; property acquired prior to marriage or by gift or inheritance is not considered in determining maintenance amount. (beginning with Sec. 30-2-50.)

Child Custody Enforcement
UCCJEA (beginning with Sec. 30-3B-101.)

Sample Caption
IN THE CIRCUIT COURT FOR _____ COUNTY, ALABAMA

IN RE THE MARRIAGE OF:)
_____,)
PETITIONER   )   Case No. _____
AND   )
_____,)
DEFENDANT.

COMPLAINT FOR DIVORCE

Alaska

Statute
Alaska Statutes beginning with Section 25.24.010.

Venue
Petition to be filed in county in which respondent lives, or, if separated, in county in which both parties resided at time of separation, or, if defendant is not a resident of Alaska, in county in which the petitioner lives. (Alaska Rule of Civil Procedure 3.)

Grounds
Irretrievable breakdown of the marriage or voluntarily living separate and apart for one year (no-fault divorce); lack of physical ability to consummate marriage; adultery; imprisonment for over two years if the total sentence is over seven years; alcoholism or drug addiction; confinement for incurable insanity for a least five years before the divorce is filed; wife is pregnant by another man at the time of the marriage without the husband's knowledge; physical abuse or reasonable fear of physical abuse; unnatural sexual behavior before or after the marriage; living separate and apart without cohabitation for over two years without the husband supporting the wife (wife must be the one filing). (Sec. 25.24.050.)

Residency
If one of the spouses is not a resident of Alaska, the spouse who files must reside in Alaska for six months prior to filing petition; if both are residents, there is no requirement. (Sec. 25.24.080.)

Property Division
Equitable distribution.

Maintenance
Marital misconduct is not a factor; property acquired before marriage is not subject to division. (Sec. 25.24.160.)

Child Custody Enforcement
UCCJEA (beginning with Sec. 25-30-300.)

Sample Caption
IN THE SUPERIOR COURT FOR THE STATE OF ALASKA
AT _____

In the Matter of the Dissolution   )
of the Marriage of   )
)
_____   )   CASE NO. _____
)
and   )
)
_____   )
Husband and Wife.   )

PETITION FOR DISSOLUTION OF MARRIAGE

Arizona

Statute
Arizona Revised Statutes beginning with Section 25-301.

Venue
Petition to be filed in the county in which the Petitioner resides.

Grounds
Irretrievable breakdown of the marriage (no-fault divorce). (Sec. 25-312.) Covenant marriage: Adultery; the respondent spouse has committed a felony and has been sentenced to death or imprisonment; the respondent spouse has abandoned the matrimonial domicile for at least one year before the petitioner filed for dissolution of marriage; the respondent spouse has physically or sexually abused the spouse seeking the dissolution of marriage, a child, or a relative of either spouse permanently living in the matrimonial domicile or has committed domestic violence or emotional abuse; the spouses have been living separate and apart continuously without reconciliation for at least two years before the petitioner filed for dissolution; the spouses have been living separate and apart continuously without reconciliation for at least one year from the date the decree of legal separation was entered; the respondent spouse has habitually abused drugs or alcohol; the parties both agree to a dissolution of marriage. (Sec. 25-903.)

Residency
Ninety days. (Sec. 25-312.)

Property Settlement
Community property (except for property acquired by gift or inheritance). (Sec. 25-211.)

Maintenance
Marital misconduct is not a factor. (Sec. 25-319.)

Child Custody Enforcement
UCCJEA (beginning with Sec. 25-1001.)

Sample Caption
SUPERIOR COURT OF ARIZONA IN _____ COUNTY

In re the marriage of)
_____,)
Petitioner,)   Case Number: _____
and)
_____,)
Respondent.

PETITION FOR DISSOLUTION OF A NON-COVENANT MARRIAGE

Arkansas

Statute
Arkansas Code beginning with Section 9-12-101.

Venue
Petition to be filed in the county in which the petitioner resides; however, if the petitioner is not a resident of the State of Arkansas and the respondent is a resident of the state, filing shall be in the county in which the respondent resides. (Sec. 9-12-303.)

Grounds
Impotence; conviction of a felony or other infamous crime; habitual drunkenness for one year; cruel and barbarous treatment as to endanger the life of the other spouse; indignities to the other as shall render his or her condition intolerable; adultery subsequent to the marriage; husband and wife have lived separate and apart from each other for eighteen continuous months without cohabitation [no-fault divorce]; husband and wife have lived separate and apart for three consecutive years without cohabitation by reason of the incurable insanity of one of them (if the insane spouse has been committed to an institution for the care and treatment of the insane for three or more years prior to the filing of the suit, has been adjudged to be of unsound mind by a court of competent jurisdiction, and has not been discharged from such adjudication by the court and the proof of insanity is supported by the evidence of two reputable physicians familiar with the mental condition of the spouse). (Sec. 9-12-301.)

In the case of a covenant marriage: adultery; commission of a felony or other infamous crime; physical or sexual abuse of the spouse or a child of one of the spouses; the parties have been living separate and apart for a period of two years; or the parties have been living separate and apart continuously without reconciliation for a period of two years from the date of judgment of judicial separation. (Sec. 9-11-808.)

Residency
Sixty days (either petitioner or respondent). (Sec. 9-12-307.)

Property Division
Equitable distribution. (Sec. 9-12-315.)

Maintenance
"The court shall make orders concerning the alimony of the wife or the husband, ... as are reasonable from the circumstances of the parties and the nature of the case." (Sec. 9-12-312.)

Child Custody Enforcement
UCCJEA (beginning with Sec. 9-19-101.)

Sample Caption
IN THE CIRCUIT COURT OF _____, ARKANSAS
DOMESTIC RELATIONS DIVISION

_____,   )
Plaintiff   )
vs.   )   No. _____
_____,   )
Defendant.   )

COMPLAINT FOR DIVORCE

California

Statute
California Family Code beginning with Section 2300.

Venue
Petition to be filed in the county in which the petitioner resides. (Sec. 2320.)

Grounds
Irreconcilable differences [no-fault divorce]; and incurable insanity. (Sec. 2310.)

Residency
Six months; and must be resident of county of filing for three months. (Sec. 2320.)

Property Division
Community property. (beginning with Sec. 2550.)

Maintenance
History of domestic violence by spouse requesting maintenance toward other spouse will preclude award of maintenance. (Sec. 4325.)

Child Custody Enforcement
UCCJEA (Sec. 3400.)

Sample Caption
SUPERIOR COURT OF CALIFORNIA, COUNTY OF _____

MARRIAGE OF

_____,
PETITIONER,
AND   CASE NUMBER: _____

_____,
RESPONDENT.

PETITION FOR DISSOLUTION OF MARRIAGE

Colorado

Statute
Colorado Revised Statutes beginning with Section 14-10-101.

Venue
Petition to be brought in the county in which the respondent resides; or, if the respondent is a nonresident, the petition may be filed where the petitioner resides. (Colorado Rule of Civil Procedure 98.)

Grounds
Irretrievable breakdown of marriage [no-fault divorce]. (Sec. 14-10-106.)

Residency
Ninety days.

Property Division
Equitable distribution. Marital misconduct is not a factor. Property acquired by gift or inheritance is not included. (Sec. 14-10-113.)

Maintenance
Marital misconduct is not considered. (Sec. 14-10-114.)

Child Custody Enforcement
UCCJEA (beginning with Sec. 14-13-101.)

Sample Caption
DISTRICT COURT, _____ COUNTY, COLORADO

In Re the Marriage of
_____

Petitioner,   CASE NUMBER: _____
and _____
Respondent.

PETITION FOR DISSOLUTION OF MARRIAGE

Connecticut

Statute
Connecticut General Statutes beginning with Section 46b-40.

Venue
Petition to be filed in the Superior Court of the judicial district in which one of the parties resides. (Sec. 46b-45.)

Grounds
The marriage has broken down irretrievably [no-fault divorce]; the parties have lived apart for the eighteen months immediately prior to the service of the petition; adultery; fraudulent contract; willful desertion for one year with total neglect of duty; seven years' absence, during all of which period the absent party has not been heard from; habitual drunkenness; intolerable cruelty; sentence of imprisonment for life or the commission of any crime punishable by imprisonment for a period in excess of one year; legal confinement in a hospital or other institution, because of mental illness, for at least five years within the period of six years preceding the date of the petition. (Sec. 46b-40.)

Residency
One year in order to obtain decree; no residency requirement to file dissolution petition. (Sec. 46b-44.)

Property Division
Equitable distribution. (Sec. 46b-81.)

Maintenance
Length of marriage and causes of dissolution may be considered. (Sec. 46b-82.)

Child Custody Enforcement
UCCJEA (beginning with Sec.46b-115.)

Sample Caption
DIVORCE COMPLAINT   STATE OF CONNECTICUT

SUPERIOR COURT

PLAINTIFF   DEFENDANT
_____   _____

Delaware

Statute
Delaware Code Title 13, beginning with Section 1501.

Venue
Petition to be filed in the county where either party resides. (Sec. 1504.)

Grounds
Irretrievable breakdown of the marriage [no-fault divorce]. "Irretrievable breakdown" caused by either voluntary separation, separation caused by respondent's misconduct, separation caused by respondent's mental illness, or separation caused by incompatibility. (Sec. 1505.)

Residency
Six months. (Sec. 1504.)

Property Division
Equitable distribution. Marital misconduct is not considered. Property acquired before marriage or by gift or inheritance is not subject to distribution. (Sec. 1513.)

Maintenance
Marital misconduct is not considered. If the marriage is for less than twenty years, duration of maintenance may not exceed 50% of length of marriage; otherwise, there is no durational limit. (Sec. 1512.)

Child Custody Enforcement
UCCJEA (beginning with Sec. 1901.)

Sample Caption
THE FAMILY COURT OF THE STATE OF DELAWARE
IN AND FOR _____ COUNTY

Petitioner,

_____,

v.   No._____, _____.

Respondent

_____.

PETITION FOR DIVORCE

District of Columbia

Statute
District of Columbia Code beginning with Section 16-901.

Venue
Family Court of the District of Columbia.

Grounds
Parties have voluntarily lived separately without cohabitation for six months; or parties have lived separately without cohabitation for one year (not necessary for both parties to agree on separation) [no-fault divorce]. (Sec. 16-904.)

Residency
Six months. (Sec. 16-902.)

Property Division
Equitable distribution. Property acquired before marriage or by gift or inheritance is not subject to distribution. (Sec. 16-910.)

Maintenance
Marital misconduct can be considered. (Sec. 16-913.)

Child Custody Enforcement
UCCJEA (beginning with Sec. 16-4601.)

Sample Caption
COURT OF THE DISTRICT OF COLUMBIA
FAMILY COURT
Domestic Relations Branch

_____
Plaintiff,
v. _____
Defendant.

COMPLAINT FOR ABSOLUTE DIVORCE

Florida

Statute
Florida Statutes beginning with Section 61.001.

Venue
Petition to be filed in the county in which the respondent resides; if respondent is a non-resident, petition to be filed in the county in which petitioner resides. (Sec. 47.011.)

Grounds
The marriage is irretrievably broken [no-fault divorce]; mental incapacity of one of the parties, if the party has been adjudged incapacitated for at least three years. (Sec. 61.052.)

Residency
Six months. (Sec. 61.021.)

Property Settlement
Equitable distribution. Property acquired before marriage or by gift or inheritance is not included. (Sec. 61.075.)

Maintenance
Adultery may be considered as a factor in awarding alimony. (Sec. 61.08.)

Child Custody Enforcement
UCCJEA (beginning with Sec. 61.501.)

Sample Caption
In the Circuit Court of the _____ Judicial Circuit
In and For _____ County, Florida

In re the marriage of   Case No.: _____
_____,   Division: _____
Petitioner,
and

_____,
Respondent.

PETITION FOR DISSOLUTION OF MARRIAGE

Georgia

Statute
Georgia Code beginning with Section 19-1-1.

Venue
Petition to be filed in the county in which the Respondent resides. (Sec. 19-5-2.)

Grounds
Intermarriage by persons within the prohibited degrees of consanguinity or affinity; mental incapacity at the time of the marriage; impotency at the time of the marriage; force, menace, duress, or fraud in obtaining the marriage; pregnancy of the wife by a man other than the husband, at the time of the marriage, unknown to the husband; adultery in either of the parties after marriage; willful and continued desertion by either of the parties for the term of one year; the conviction of either party for an offense involving moral turpitude, under which he is sentenced to imprisonment in a penal institution for a term of two years or longer; habitual intoxication; cruel treatment (willful infliction of pain such as reasonably justifies apprehension of danger to life, limb, or health); incurable mental illness; habitual drug addiction; the marriage is irretrievably broken [no-fault divorce]. (Sec. 19-5-3.)

Residency
Six months. (Sec. 19-5-2.)

Property Division
Equitable distribution. Marital misconduct may be considered.

Maintenance
Adultery and desertion are factors prohibiting an award of alimony. (Sec. 19-6-1.) Cohabitation with another by recipient spouse requires termination of maintenance. (Sec. 19-6-12.)

Child Custody Enforcement
UCCJEA (beginning with Sec. 19-9-101.)

Sample Caption
IN THE SUPERIOR COURT OF _____ COUNTY
STATE OF GEORGIA

_____
Plaintiff,
vs.   CASE NUMBER _____

_____
Defendant.
COMPLAINT FOR DIVORCE

Hawaii

Statute
Hawaii Revised Statutes beginning with Section 580-1.

Venue
Petition to be filed in the county in which petitioner resides. (Sec. 580-1.)

Grounds
The marriage is irretrievably broken [no-fault divorce]; the parties have lived separate and apart under a separation decree and no reconciliation has been effected; the parties have lived separate and apart for a period of two years or more under a decree of separate maintenance entered by any court of competent jurisdiction, and no reconciliation has been effected; or the parties have lived separate and apart for a continuous period of two years or more immediately preceding the application, there is no reasonable likelihood that cohabitation will be resumed. (Sec. 580-41.)

Residency
Three months for filing, six months for decree of dissolution may be granted. (Sec. 580-1.)

Property Settlement
Equitable distribution. (Sec. 580-47.)

Maintenance
Marital misconduct is not considered. (Sec. 580-47.)

Child Custody Enforcement
UCCJEA (Sec. 583A-101.)

Sample Caption
IN THE FAMILY COURT OF THE _____ CIRCUIT
STATE OF HAWAII

COMPLAINT FOR DIVORCE

_____,
Plaintiff,
v.
_____,
Defendant.

Idaho

Statute
Idaho Statutes beginning with Section 32-601.

Venue
Petition to be filed in the county in which defendant resides; if defendant is not a resident, then in whatever county the plaintiff designates. (Sec. 5-404.)

Grounds
Adultery; extreme cruelty; willful desertion; willful neglect; habitual intemperance; conviction of felony; when either the husband or wife has become permanently insane; irreconcilable differences [no-fault divorce]. (Sec. 32-603.)

Residency
Six weeks. (Sec. 32-701.)

Property Settlement
Community property. (Sec. 32-712.) Property acquired prior to marriage, or by gift or inheritance, is not included.

Maintenance
Marital fault may be considered. (Sec. 32-705.)

Child Custody Enforcement
UCCJEA (Sec. 32-11-101.)

Sample Caption
IN THE DISTRICT COURT OF THE _____ JUDICIAL DISTRICT OF THE
STATE OF IDAHO, IN AND FOR THE COUNTY OF _____

_____,   :)
Plaintiff,   :)
vs.   :)   Case No. _____
_____,   :)
Defendant.   :)

COMPLAINT FOR DIVORCE

Illinois

Statute
750 Illinois Compiled Statutes beginning with 5/101.

Venue
Petition to be filed in the county in which either the plaintiff or defendant reside. (Sec. 5/104.)

Grounds
Impotence; bigamy; adultery; desertion for one year; habitual drunkenness for two years; excessive drug use of two years; attempt on the life of the petitioner showing malice; physical or mental cruelty; conviction of a felony or other infamous crime; respondent has infected petitioner with a sexually transmitted disease; the spouses have lived separate and apart for two years and irreconcilable differences have caused the irretrievable breakdown of the marriage [no-fault divorce]. If the spouses have lived apart for six months, the two-year requirement may be waived in a writing filed with the court. (Sec. 5/401.)

Residency
Ninety days. (Sec. 5/401.)

Property Division
Marital misconduct is not a factor in division of property. Property acquired prior to marriage or by gift or inheritance is excluded. (Sec. 5/503.)

Maintenance
Marital misconduct is not a factor in determining an award. (Sec. 5/504.)

Child Custody Enforcement
UCCJEA (beginning with Sec. 36/101.)

Sample Caption
IN THE CIRCUIT COURT OF THE _____ JUDICIAL CIRCUIT _____ COUNTY, ILLINOIS

IN RE THE MARRIAGE OF:

_____,   )
Petitioner,   )
and   )   Case No. _____
_____,   )
Respondent.   )

PETITION FOR DISSOLUTION OF MARRIAGE

Indiana

Statute
Indiana Code beginning with Section 31-15-1-1.

Venue
Petition to be filed in the county in which one of the parties has resided for three months. (Sec. 31-15-2-6.)

Grounds
Irretrievable breakdown of the marriage [no-fault divorce]; conviction of either of the parties of a felony; impotence at the time of the marriage; incurable insanity of either party for two years. (Sec. 31-15-2-3.)

Residency
Six months. (Sec. 31-15-2-6.)

Property Division
Equitable distribution. Marital misconduct is not a factor. Property acquired by a party before marriage is subject to distribution. (Sec. 31-15-7-4.)

Maintenance
Marital misconduct is not a factor. (Sec. 31-15-7-1.)

Child Custody Enforcement
UCCJA (Sec. 31-17-3.)

Sample Caption
STATE OF INDIANA)   IN THE _____ COURT) SS.
COUNTY OF _____)   CASE NO. _____

IN RE THE MARRIAGE OF:

_____,
Petitioner,
and

_____,
Respondent.

VERIFIED PETITION FOR DISSOLUTION OF MARRIAGE

Iowa

Statute
Iowa Code beginning with Section 598.1.

Venue
Petition to be filed in the county in which either party resides. (Sec. 598.2.)

Grounds
"[B]reakdown of the marriage relationship to the extent that the legitimate objects of matrimony have been destroyed and there remains no reasonable likelihood that the marriage can be preserved [no-fault divorce]." (Sec. 598.17.)

Residency
No requirement if respondent is a resident; otherwise, petitioner must be a resident for one year. (Sec. 598.2.)

Property Division
Equitable distribution. Marital misconduct is not a factor. Property acquired by a party by gift or inheritance is subject to division. (Sec. 598.21.)

Maintenance
Fault is not considered. (Sec. 598.21A.)

Child Custody Enforcement
UCCJEA (beginning with Sec. 598B.101.)

Sample Caption
Petition for Dissolution of Marriage
In the District Court of the State of Iowa In and For _____ County

In Re the Marriage of
_____ and _____

Upon the Petition for Dissolution of Marriage

_____
(Petitioner)

and

_____
(Respondent)

Kansas

Statute
Kansas Statutes beginning with Section 60-1601.

Venue
Petition to be filed in the county in which either party resides. (Sec. 60-607.)

Grounds
Incompatibility; failure to perform a material marital duty or obligation; or mental illness or mental incapacity of one or both spouses. (Sec. 60-1601.)

Residency
Sixty days. (Sec. 60-1603.)

Property Division
Equitable jurisdiction. Property acquired prior to marriage or by gift or inheritance is subject to division. (Sec. 60-1610.)

Maintenance
May not be awarded for a period in excess of 121 months, although under certain circumstances may be reinstated. (Sec. 60-1610.)

Child Custody Enforcement
UCCJEA (Sec. 38-1336.)

Sample Caption
PETITION FOR DIVORCE

IN THE DISTRICT COURT IN AND FOR THE COUNTY OF _____, KANSAS

In re: the Marriage of
_____

and
_____

)
)
)
) Docket No._____
)

Kentucky

Statute
Kentucky Revised Statutes beginning with Section 403.00.

Venue
Petition to be filed in the county in which either party resides. (Sec. 452.470.)

Grounds
Irretrievable breakdown of marriage. (Sec. 403.170.)

Residency
180 days. (Sec. 403.140.)

Property Division
Marital misconduct not a factor. Property acquired prior to marriage or by gift or inheritance is not subject to distribution. (Sec. 403.190.)

Maintenance
Marital misconduct not a factor. (Sec. 403.200.)

Child Custody Enforcement
UCCJEA (beginning with Sec. 403.800.)

Sample Caption
COMMONWEALTH OF KENTUCKY
COURT OF JUSTICE

PETITION FOR DISSOLUTION OF MARRIAGE
IN RE THE MARRIAGE OF

_____,
Petitioner,
and

_____,
Respondent.

Louisiana

Statute
Louisiana Civil Code Art. 101.

Venue
Petition to be brought in the parish in which either party resides, or the last parish in which both parties resided before separation. (Civil Code Art. 3941.)

Grounds
Parties have been living apart continuously for 180 days if there are no minor children, or 365 days if there are minor children; adultery; or the other spouse has committed a felony and has been sentenced to death or imprisonment at hard labor. (Civil Code Art. 103.) In the case of covenant marriage, the parties must first undergo counseling, and one of the following grounds must exist: adultery; spouse has committed a felony and has been sentenced to death or imprisonment at hard labor; abandonment for one year; physical or sexual abuse; the parties have been living separate and apart for two years; or the parties have been living separate and apart for one year after separation decree is signed. (Louisiana Revised Statutes Sec. 9:272.)

Residency
Six months. (Code of Civil Procedure Art. 10.)

Property Division
Community property. (Civil Code Art. 2334.)

Maintenance
Marital fault is a bar to award of maintenance. (Civil Code Art. 111.)

Child Custody Enforcement
UCCJA (until August 15, 2007) (Louisiana Revised Statutes Sec. 13:1700); UCCJEA (effective August 15, 2007) (Louisiana Revised Statutes Sec. 13:1801)

Sample Caption
District Court for the Parish of _____
State of Louisiana

_____,
Petitioner,
vs.

_____,
Respondent.

PETITION FOR DIVORCE

Maine

Statute
Maine Revised Statutes Title 19, Chapter 13, beginning with Section 631.

Venue
Petition to be filed in the county in which either party resides. (Sec. 155.)

Grounds
Adultery; impotence; extreme cruelty; desertion for three years; habitual intoxication from drugs or alcohol; nonsupport; cruel and abusive treatment; irreconcilable differences [no-fault divorce]; or mental illness requiring confinement for seven years. (Sec. 902.)

Residency
Six months. In the alternative, residency is met if the petitioner resides in the state and the parties were married there, or if the petitioner resides in the state and the cause of the divorce occurred in the state; or if the respondent resides in the state. (Sec. 901.)

Property Division
Equitable distribution. Property acquired before marriage or by gift or inheritance is not subject to division. Marital misconduct is not considered. (Sec. 953.)

Maintenance
There is a presumption that permanent maintenance may not be awarded if the parties were married for less than ten years, and a presumption that it may not be awarded for a term greater than half as long as the marriage if the parties were married between ten and twenty years. (Sec. 951-A.)

Child Custody Enforcement
UCCJEA (Sec. 1731.)

Sample Caption
State of Maine
District Court
Location:_____
Docket No. _____

_____,
Plaintiff
v.   Complaint for Divorce
_____,
Defendant.

Maryland

Statute
Maryland Code Family Law Article, beginning with Section 7-101.

Venue
Petition to be filed in the county in which either party resides. (Courts and Judicial Proceedings Article, Secs. 6-201 and 6-202.)

Grounds
Adultery; desertion for twelve months; voluntary separation for twelve months [no-fault ground]; conviction of felony or misdemeanor with sentence of at least three years; separation for two years [no-fault ground]; insanity, if the insane spouse is institutionalized for at least three years; cruelty toward the petitioner or petitioner's child; excessively vicious conduct toward the petitioner or petitioner's child. (Family Law Article, Sec. 7-103.)

Residency
No time requirement if the cause of the divorce arose in the state; otherwise, one year. (Family Law Article, Sec. 7-101.)

Property Division
Equitable distribution. Marital misconduct may be a factor. Property acquired prior to marriage or by gift or inheritance is not subject to distribution. (Family Law Article, Sec. 8-205.)

Maintenance
Marital misconduct may be considered. (Family Law Article, Sec. 11-106.)

Child Custody Enforcement
UCCJEA (Family Law Article, Sec. 9.5-101.)

Sample Caption
CIRCUIT COURT FOR _____, MARYLAND
CASE NO._____

_____.
Defendant

_____
Plaintiff

Massachusetts

Statute
Massachusetts General Laws, Chapter 208, beginning with Section 1.

Venue
Petition to be filed in the county in which the parties last cohabited, if one party still resides in the county; otherwise, in the county in which either party resides. (Sec. 6.)

Grounds
Adultery; impotency; desertion for one year; habitual intoxication; abusive treatment; nonsupport; irretrievable breakdown of the marriage [no-fault divorce], incarceration for five years or more. (Sec. 1, 1A, 1B, 2.)

Residency
None, if grounds occurred in state; otherwise one year. (Secs. 4, 5.)

Property Division
Equitable distribution. Marital misconduct may be considered. (Sec. 34.)

Maintenance
Marital misconduct may be considered. (Sec. 34.)

Child Custody Enforcement
UCCJA (Chap. 209B, Sec.1.)

Sample Caption
COMMONWEALTH OF MASSACHUSETTS
THE TRIAL COURT
PROBATE AND FAMILY COURT DEPARTMENT
Docket No. _____

COMPLAINT FOR DIVORCE

_____, Plaintiff
v.
_____, Defendant.

Michigan

Statute
Michigan Compiled Laws Chapter 552.

Venue
Petition to be filed in the county in which either party resides, if the party has resided in that county for ten days prior to filing. (Sec. 552.9.)

Grounds
Breakdown of the marriage with no reasonable likelihood of preserving the marriage [no-fault divorce]. (Sec. 552.6.)

Residency
180 days. (Sec. 552.9.)

Property Division
Equitable distribution. (Sec. 552.19.) The court may render "a further judgment for restoring to either party the whole, or such parts as it shall deem just and reasonable, of the real and personal estate that shall have come to either party by reason of the marriage..."

Maintenance
Alimony sufficient for the maintenance of the other party may be ordered. (Sec. 552.13.)

Child Custody Enforcement
UCCJEA (beginning with Sec. 722.1101.)

Sample Caption
STATE OF MICHIGAN
_____ JUDICIAL CIRCUIT
_____ COUNTY

COMPLAINT FOR DIVORCE

_____,
Plaintiff,
v.

_____,
Defendant.

Minnesota

Statute
Minnesota Statutes beginning with Section 518.002.

Venue
Petition is to be filed in the county in which either party resides. (Sec. 518.09.)

Grounds
Irretrievable breakdown of the marriage [no-fault divorce]. (Sec. 518.06.)

Residency
180 days. (Sec. 518.07.)

Property Division
Equitable distribution. Property acquired prior to marriage, or by gift or inheritance, is not subject to distribution. (Sec. 518.54.) Marital misconduct is not considered. (Sec. 518.58.)

Maintenance
Marital misconduct not considered. (Sec. 518.552.)

Child Custody Enforcement
UCCJEA (beginning with Sec. 518D.101.)

Sample Caption
STATE OF MINNESOTA   DISTRICT COURT
COUNTY OF _____   JUDICIAL DISTRICT: _____
COURT FILE NUMBER: _____

IN RE THE MARRIAGE OF:
PETITION FOR DISSOLUTION OF MARRIAGE

_____,
Petitioner,
and

_____,
Respondent.

Mississippi

Statute
Mississippi Code beginning with Section 93-5-1.

Venue
No-fault petitions to be filed in the county in which either party resides. All other petitions to be filed either in the county in which the respondent resides or in the last counties in which the parties lived together; if the respondent is not a resident, the petition is to be filed in the county in which the petitioner resides. (Sec. 93-5-11.)

Grounds
Impotency; adultery; sentence to penitentiary; willful desertion for one year; habitual drunkenness; habitual drug use; habitual cruel and inhuman treatment; insanity at the time of the marriage, if unknown to the other party; bigamy; pregnancy of wife by another man at the time of the marriage, if unknown by the husband; consanguinity; incurable insanity after treatment for such for three years; irreconcilable differences [no-fault divorce]. (Sec. 93-5-2.)

Residency
Six months. (Sec. 93-5-5.)

Property Division
Equitable distribution. Discretionary with the court.

Maintenance
Discretionary with the court. (Sec. 93-5-23.)

Child Custody Enforcement
UCCJEA (Sec. 93-27-101.)

Sample Caption
CHANCERY COURT OF _____ COUNTY
STATE OF MISSISSIPPI

BILL OF COMPLAINT OF DIVORCE

_____,
Complainant,
v.

_____,
Defendant.

Missouri

Statute
Missouri Revised Statute beginning with Section 452.025.

Venue
Petition to be filed in the county in which either party resides. (Sec. 452.300.)

Grounds
Marriage is irretrievably broken [no-fault divorce]. (Sec. 452.305.)

Residency
Ninety days for filing; thirty more days for entry of judgment of dissolution. (Sec. 452.305.)

Property Division
Equitable distribution. Property acquired before the marriage, or by gift or inheritance, is not subject to division. (Sec. 452.330.)

Maintenance
Marital misconduct may be considered. (Sec. 452.335.)

Child Custody Enforcement
UCCJA (beginning with Sec. 452.440.)

Sample Caption
IN THE CIRCUIT COURT OF _____ COUNTY, MISSOURI

IN RE THE MARRIAGE OF

_____,
PETITIONER,
AND

_____,
RESPONDENT.

PETITION FOR DISSOLUTION OF MARRIAGE

Montana

Statute
Montana Code Annotated beginning with Section 40-4-101.

Venue
Petition to be filed in the county in which either party resides. (Sec. 25-2-118.)

Grounds
Irretrievable breakdown of marriage [no-fault divorce]. (Sec. 40-4-107.)

Residency
Ninety days. (Sec. 40-4-104.)

Property Division
Equitable distribution. Marital misconduct is not a factor. All property belonging to the parties are subject to division. (Sec. 40-4-202.)

Maintenance
Marital misconduct is not considered. (Sec. 40-4-203.)

Child Custody Enforcement
UCCJEA (beginning with Sec. 40-7-101.)

Sample Caption
MONTANA, _____ JUDICIAL DISTRICT COURT

IN RE THE MARRIAGE OF: CAUSE NO. _____

_____,
Petitioner,   Judge _____
and
_____,   PETITION FOR DISSOLUTION
Respondent.   OF MARRIAGE

Nebraska

Statute
Nebraska Statutes beginning with Section 42-341.

Venue
Petition to be brought in the county in which either party resides. (Sec. 42-348.)

Grounds
Marriage is irretrievably broken [no-fault divorce]. (Sec. 42-361.)

Residency
No residency requirement if the marriage was entered into in state, and one party has resided within the state for the entire length of the marriage; otherwise, one year. (Sec. 42-342.)

Property Division
Equitable distribution. In general, all property acquired during the marriage by either spouse is subject to division, but in practice, that acquired by gift or inheritance often will not be divided. (Sec. 42-365.)

Maintenance
Marital misconduct is not considered. (Sec. 42-365.)

Child Custody Enforcement
UCCJEA (beginning with Sec. 43-1226.)

Sample Caption
IN THE DISTRICT COURT OF _____ COUNTY, NEBRASKA

_____,)	Case No. _____	
Plaintiff,)		
vs.)	COMPLAINT FOR DISSOLUTION	
_____,)	OF MARRIAGE	
Defendant.)		

Nevada

Statute
Nevada Revised Statutes beginning with Section 125.005.

Venue
Petition to be filed in the county either: where either party resides, where the cause of the divorce occurred, or in which the parties last cohabited. (Sec. 125.020.)

Grounds
Insanity of one party for two years prior to filing; parties living separate and apart for one year [no-fault divorce]; incompatibility [no-fault divorce]. (Sec. 125.010.)

Residency
Six weeks. (Sec 125.020.)

Property Division
Community property. Property acquired prior to marriage, in a personal injury case, or by gift or inheritance is excluded from community. (Secs. 123.130, 125.150.)

Maintenance
No enumerated statutory factors, except that the court may order alimony for purpose of obtaining education and training. (Sec. 125.150.)

Child Custody Enforcement
UCCJEA (Sec. 125A.015.)

Sample Caption
DISTRICT COURT

_____ COUNTY, NEVADA

_____,	)	Case No. _____
Plaintiff,	)	
vs.	)	Dept. No. _____
_____,	)	
Defendant.	)	

COMPLAINT FOR DIVORCE

New Hampshire

Statute
New Hampshire Revised Statutes beginning with Section 458.1.

Venue
Petition to be filed in the county in which either party resides. (Sec. 458:9.)

Grounds
Impotency; adultery; extreme cruelty; conviction of a crime punishable with imprisonment for more than one year and actual imprisonment under such conviction; treatment of the other as seriously to injure physical or emotional health; either party has been absent two years together; habitual drunkenness for two years; membership in a religion or other organization that considers the marriage to be unlawful, along with refusal to cohabit with the other for six months; abandonment for two years; irreconcilable differences [no-fault divorce]. (Sec. 458:7-a.)

Residency
One year. (Sec. 458:5.)

Property Division
Equitable distribution. Marital misconduct may be considered. All property is subject to division. (Sec. 458:16-a.)

Maintenance
Marital misconduct may be considered. (Sec. 458.19.)

Child Custody Enforcement
UCCJA (beginning with Sec. 458-A:1.)

Sample Caption
THE STATE OF NEW HAMPSHIRE
JUDICIAL BRANCH
COURT NAME: _____
CASE NAME: _____
CASE NO.: _____

_____
Petitioner

_____
Respondent

New Jersey

Statute
New Jersey Permanent Statutes beginning with Section 2A:34-1.

Venue
Petition to be filed in any county in the state. (Sec. 2A:34-8)

Grounds
Adultery; desertion for one year; extreme cruelty; separation for eighteen months [no-fault divorce]; habitual drunkenness or drug addiction for twelve months; institutionalization for mental illness for twenty-four months; imprisonment for eighteen months; deviant sexual conduct by one party without the approval of the other party. (Sec. 2A:34-2.)

Residency
No time limit if grounds are adultery and one party was at the time the grounds occurred and currently is a resident; otherwise, one year. (Sec. 2A:34-10.)

Property Division
Equitable distribution. Property acquired prior to marriage or by gift or inheritance is not subject to division. (Sec. 2A:34-23.1.)

Maintenance
Court may order: permanent alimony; rehabilitative alimony; limited duration alimony or reimbursement alimony to either party. (Sec. 2A:34-23.)

Child Custody Enforcement
UCCJEA (beginning with Sec. 2A:34-53.)

Sample Caption _____
SUPERIOR COURT OF NEW JERSEY CHANCERY DIVISION
Plaintiff,   FAMILY PART
vs.   _____ COUNTY
_____   Docket No. _____
Defendant.   VERIFIED COMPLAINT FOR DIVORCE

New Mexico

Statute
New Mexico Annotated Statutes beginning with Section 40-4-1.

Venue
Petition to be filed in the county in which either party resides. (Sec. 40-4-4.)

Grounds
Incompatibility [no-fault divorce]; cruel and inhuman treatment; adultery; abandonment. (Sec. 40-4-1.)

Residency
Six months. (Sec. 40-4-5.)

Property Division
Property acquired prior to marriage, or by gift or inheritance is not subject to division. (Sec. 40-3-8.)

Maintenance
Statutory factors are provided. (Sec. 40-4-7.)

Child Custody Enforcement
UCCJEA (Sec. 40-10A-101.)

Sample Caption
STATE OF NEW MEXICO
COUNTY OF _____
_____ JUDICIAL DISTRICT

- -
Petitioner

v.   No. _____

- -
Respondent

VERIFIED PETITION FOR DISSOLUTION OF MARRIAGE

New York

Statute
Laws of New York Domestic Relations, Article 10.

Venue
Petition to be filed in the county in which either party resides. (Laws of New York, Civil Practice Law and Rules, Sec. 503.)

Grounds
Cruel and inhuman treatment; abandonment for one year; imprisonment for three or more years; adultery; parties have lived apart pursuant to court order of separation for one year or more [no-fault divorce]; parties have lived apart for one year or more pursuant to a written agreement [no-fault divorce]. (Sec. 170.)

Residency
No residency requirement if the cause of the divorce occurred in state and both parties were residents at the time of the commencement of the action. One year, if: the parties were married in state; or the parties have resided in state as husband and wife; or the cause of the divorce occurred in state. Otherwise, two years. (Sec. 230.)

Property Division
Equitable distribution. Property acquired before the marriage, as compensation for personal injury; or by gift or inheritance, is not marital property subject to division. (Sec. 236.)

Maintenance
Statutory factors are in Sec. 236.

Child Custody Enforcement
UCCJEA (beginning with Sec. 75.)

Sample Caption
SUPREME COURT OF THE STATE OF NEW YORK
COUNTY OF _____

_____   Index No.:

Plaintiff,
-against-

_____   VERIFIED COMPLAINT
                              ACTION FOR DIVORCE
Defendant.

North Carolina

Statute
North Carolina General Statutes beginning with Section 50-2.

Venue
Petition to be filed in the county in which either party resides. (Sec. 50-3.)

Grounds
Incurable insanity; separation for one year [no-fault divorce]. (Sec. 50-5.1, 50-6.)

Residency
Six months. (Sec. 50-6.)

Property Division
Equitable distribution. (Sec. 50-20.) Property acquired prior to marriage, or by gift or inheritance, is not subject to division.

Maintenance
Marital misconduct is a factor. Adultery by a party seeking alimony will bar award of alimony. (Sec. 50-16.3A.)

Child Custody Enforcement
UCCJEA (Chap. 50A.)

Sample Caption

STATE OF NORTH CAROLINA

_____ County

File No._____

In the General Court of Justice
District Court Division

_____

Plaintiff,

v.

_____

Defendant.

JUDGMENT FOR ABSOLUTE DIVORCE
BEFORE THE COURT

North Dakota

Statute
North Dakota Century Code beginning with Section 14-05-01.

Venue
Petition to be filed in the county in which the respondent resides; if respondent is not a resident, then in any county of petitioner's choosing. (Sec. 28-04-05.)

Grounds
Adultery; extreme cruelty; willful desertion; willful neglect; drug or alcohol abuse; conviction of felony; irreconcilable differences [no-fault divorce]. (Sec. 14-05-03.)

Residency
Six months. (Sec. 14-05-17.)

Property Division
Equitable distribution. (Sec. 14-05-24.)

Maintenance
No statutory factors are given; alimony is awarded by "taking into consideration the circumstances of the parties". (Sec. 14-05-24.1.)

Child Custody Enforcement
UCCJEA (Sec. 14-14.1.)

Sample Caption
IN DISTRICT COURT, _____ COUNTY, NORTH DAKOTA

_____)
Plaintiff,   )   COMPLAINT FOR DIVORCE
v.   )
_____)   Civil No. _____
Defendant.   )

Ohio

Statute
Ohio Revised Code beginning with Chapter 3105.01.

Venue
Petition to be filed in the county in which the plaintiff has resided for at least ninety days. (Ohio Rule of Civil Procedure 3.)

Grounds
Bigamy; desertion for one year; adultery; extreme cruelty; fraud in obtaining the marriage; neglect; habitual drunkenness; imprisonment; obtaining a divorce in another state that does not release the respondent from marital obligations; living separately for one year [no-fault divorce]; incompatibility [no-fault divorce]. (Sec. 3105.01.)

Residency
Six months. (Sec. 3105.03.)

Property Division
Equitable distribution. Property that is acquired prior to the marriage, as compensation for personal injury, or by gift or inheritance, is not subject to division. (Sec. 3105.171.)

Maintenance
Statutory factors are found at Section 3105.18.

Child Custody Enforcement
UCCJEA (beginning with Sec. 3127.01.)

Sample Caption
COURT OF COMMON PLEAS
DIVISION OF DOMESTIC RELATIONS
_____ COUNTY, OHIO

_____   Case No. _____

Petitioner,
v.   COMPLAINT FOR DISSOLUTION
_____   OF MARRIAGE

Petitioner.

Oklahoma

Statute
Oklahoma Statutes beginning with Section 43-1.

Venue
Petition to be filed in the county in which petitioner has resided for thirty days, or the county in which the respondent resides. (Sec. 43-103.)

Grounds
Abandonment for one year; adultery; impotency; pregnancy of wife by another at the time of the marriage; extreme cruelty; fraudulent contract; incompatibility [no-fault divorce]; habitual drunkenness; gross neglect; imprisonment for a felony; obtaining a divorce that does not release the other spouse from marital obligations; insanity for five years. (Sec. 43-101.)

Residency
Six months. (Sec. 43-102.)

Property Division
Equitable distribution. The standard provided in the statute is that the division be "just and reasonable." (Sec. 43-121.)

Maintenance
"[S]uch alimony…as the court shall think reasonable. (Sec. 43-121.)

Child Custody Enforcement
UCCJEA (Sec. 43-551-102.)

Sample Caption
IN THE DISTRICT COURT OF _____ COUNTY
STATE OF OKLAHOMA

PLAINTIFF
_____

v.   CASE NO. _____
DEFENDANT
_____

Oregon

Statute
Oregon Revised Statutes beginning with Section 107.005.

Venue
Petition to be filed in the county in which either party resides. (Sec. 107.086.)

Grounds
One of the parties was a minor at the time of the marriage; one of the parties had insufficient mental capacity to consent to the marriage; consent was obtained by force or fraud; irreconcilable differences [no-fault divorce]. (Sec. 107.015.)

Residency
Six months. (Sec. 107.075.) Also, there is a ninety-day waiting period after filing before a hearing or trial can be scheduled. (Sec. 107.065.)

Property Division
Equitable distribution. (Sec. 107.105.) Marital misconduct is not considered. (Sec. 107.036.)

Maintenance
Fault is not considered. (Sec. 107.036.)

Child Custody Enforcement
UCCJEA (Sec. 109.701.)

Sample Caption
IN THE CIRCUIT COURT OF THE STATE OF OREGON
FOR THE COUNTY OF _____

In the Matter of the Marriage of
_____   Case No. _____

Petitioner,
v.   PETITION FOR DISSOLUTION
_____   OF MARRIAGE
Respondent.

Pennsylvania

Statute
Pennsylvania Consolidated Statutes Title 23, beginning with Section 3101.

Venue
Petition to be filed in the county in which the respondent resides; or, if the respondent resides out of state, where the plaintiff resides; or, if the plaintiff has continuously resided in the county, in the county of both parties' residence during the marriage; or, if respondent agrees, the county in which the petitioner resides; or, if neither party resides in the county of matrimonial domicile or if the parties have been separated for six months, the county in which either party resides. (Sec. 3104.)

Grounds
Desertion for one year; adultery; cruelty; bigamy; sentence of imprisonment for two or more years; indignities; institutionalization in a mental health facility for 18 months or more; mutual consent and 90 days' separation [no-fault divorce]; irretrievable breakdown of marriage [no-fault divorce]. (Sec. 3301.)

Residency
Six months. (Sec. 3104.)

Property Division
Equitable distribution. Fault is not considered. (Sec. 3502.) Property acquired before the marriage or by gift or inheritance is not subject to division. (Sec. 3501.)

Maintenance
Fault may be considered. (Sec. 3701.)

Child Custody Enforcement
UCCJA (beginning with Sec. 5341.)

Sample Caption
IN THE COURT OF COMMON PLEAS FOR _____ COUNTY, PENNSYLVANIA
FAMILY DIVISION

_____

Plaintiff,
v.   Case Number: FD _____

_____

Defendant.

COMPLAINT FOR DIVORCE

Rhode Island

Statute
Rhode Island General Laws beginning with Section 15-5-1.

Venue
Petition to be filed in the county in which petitioner resides; if petition is based upon residence of respondent, then in the county in which defendant resides or in Providence County. (Sec. 15-5-13.)

Grounds
Impotency; adultery; extreme cruelty; willful desertion; habitual drunkenness or drug use; neglect for one year; gross misbehavior; irreconcilable differences. (Sec. 15-5-3.1.)

Residency
One year. (Sec. 15-5-12.)

Property Division
Equitable distribution. Marital misconduct may be considered. Property acquired before marriage or by gift or inheritance is not subject to division. (Sec. 15-5-16.1.)

Maintenance
Marital misconduct may be considered. (Sec. 15-5-16.)

Child Custody Enforcement
UCCJEA (beginning with Sec. 15-14.1-1.)

Sample Caption
STATE OF RHODE ISLAND FAMILY COURT

_____

Petitioner,

v.   Case No. _____

_____

Respondent.

South Carolina

Statute
South Carolina Code of Laws beginning with Section 20-1-10.

Venue
Petition to be filed either: in the county in which respondent resides; or if respondent is a nonresident, then in the county in which petitioner resides; or the county in which the parties last resided together as husband and wife. (Sec. 20-3-60.)

Grounds
Adultery; desertion for one year; physical cruelty; habitual drunkenness or drug use; living separate and apart for one year [no-fault divorce]. (Sec. 20-3-10.)

Residency
One year if one of parties is a resident; if both parties are residents, then petitioner is only required to have resided in state for three months. (Sec. 20-3-30.)

Property Division
Equitable distribution. Property acquired prior to marriage, or by gift or inheritance, is not subject to division. Marital misconduct is considered. (Sec. 20-7-472.)

Maintenance
Marital misconduct may be considered; alimony is not to be awarded to a party who committed adultery. (Sec. 20-3-130.)

Child Custody Enforcement
UCCJA (beginning with Sec. 20-7-782.)

Sample Caption
COMPLAINT FOR DIVORCE

_____
Plaintiff,
v.   Case No. _____

_____
Defendant.

South Dakota

Statute
South Dakota Codified Laws beginning with Section 25-1-1.

Venue
Petition to be filed in the county in which either party resides; however, respondent may move to have the case transferred to the respondent's county. (Sec. 25-4-30.1.)

Grounds
Adultery; extreme cruelty; willful desertion; willful neglect; habitual drunkenness; conviction of felony; irreconcilable differences [no-fault divorce]. (Sec. 25-4-2.)

Residency
None, but petitioner must be a resident from the time of filing until the decree of dissolution is entered. (Sec. 25-4-30.)

Property Division
Equitable distribution. No statutory factors, but fault is not considered. (Sec. 25-4-45.1.)

Maintenance
No statutory factors. (Sec. 25-4-41.)

Child Custody Enforcement
UCCJEA (beginning with Sec. 26-5B-101.)

Sample Caption
STATE OF SOUTH DAKOTA, COUNTY OF _____
IN CIRCUIT COURT _____ JUDICIAL DISTRICT

In Re: The Marriage of)
_____) CASE NO. _____

Plaintiff,)
and)
_____) COMPLAINT FOR DIVORCE

Defendant.)

Tennessee

Statute
Tennessee Code beginning with Section 36-4-101.

Venue
Petition to be filed in the county in which the parties reside at the time of separation, or in the county in which respondent resides; however, if the respondent is a nonresident, then in the county in which petitioner resides. (Sec. 36-4-105.)

Grounds
Impotence; bigamy; adultery; willful desertion for one year; conviction of an infamous crime; conviction and imprisonment for a felony; attempt on the spouse's life; remaining willfully absent from the state for two years; pregnancy by another man at the time of the marriage; habitual drunkenness or drug abuse; cruel and inhuman treatment; intolerable indignities; abandonment or turning out of doors; irreconcilable differences [no-fault divorce]; living in separate residences for two years [no-fault divorce]. (Sec. 36-4-101.)

Residency
Six months. (Sec. 36-4-104.)

Property Division
Equitable distribution. Marital misconduct is not considered. Property acquired prior to marriage, by gift or inheritance, or as compensation for personal injury or victim's compensation is not subject to distribution. (Sec. 36-4-121.)

Maintenance
Marital misconduct can be considered in awarding alimony. (Sec. 36-5-121.)

Child Custody Enforcement
UCCJEA (Sec. 36-6-201.)

Sample Caption
IN THE _____[CIRCUIT/CHANCERY] COURT
OF _____COUNTY, TENNESSEE

_____,
Petitioner,
v.   CIVIL ACTION DOCKET NO. _____

_____,
Respondent.

COMPLAINT OF DIVORCE

Texas

Statute
Texas Statutes Family Code beginning with Section 6.001.

Venue
Petition to be filed in the county in which respondent resides. (Sec. 15.082.)

Grounds
Conflict of personalities [no-fault divorce]; cruelty; adultery; conviction of felony and imprisonment for one year; abandonment; living apart for three years [no-fault divorce]; confinement in mental hospital for three years. (Secs. 6.001-6.007.)

Residency
Six months in state; ninety days in the county of filing. (Sec. 6.301.)

Property Division
Community property. (beginning with Sec. 3.001.) Property acquired prior to marriage, by gift or inheritance, or as compensation for personal injury is not community property or subject to division.

Maintenance
Marital misconduct of the spouse seeking alimony is a factor. (Sec. 8.052.)

Child Custody Enforcement
UCCJEA (beginning with Sec. 152.001.)

Sample Caption
IN THE MATTER OF THE MARRIAGE OF IN THE DISTRICT
COURT OF_____ COUNTY

_____,)
Petitioner,)
and)
_____,)   #_____
Respondent.)

Utah

Statute
Utah Code Annotated beginning with Section 30-3-1.

Venue
Petition to be filed in the county in which petitioner resides.

Grounds
Impotency; adultery; willful desertion for more than one year; willful neglect; habitual drunkenness; conviction for a felony; cruel treatment; irreconcilable differences [no-fault divorce]; incurable insanity; or when the husband and wife have lived separately for three years [no-fault divorce]. (Sec. 30-3-1.)

Residency
Three months. (Sec. 30-3-1.)

Property Division
Equitable distribution. (Sec. 30-3-5.) Marital misconduct is considered.

Maintenance
Marital misconduct may be considered. Alimony may not be ordered for a period longer than the duration of the marriage, absent extenuating circumstances. (Sec. 30-3-5.)

Child Custody Enforcement
UCCJEA (beginning with Sec. 78-45c-101.)

Sample Caption
IN THE _____ JUDICIAL DISTRICT COURT
_____ COUNTY, UTAH

_____,

Petitioner,   COMPLAINT FOR DIVORCE
vs.

_____, CASE NO. _____

Respondent.

Vermont

Statute
Vermont Statutes Title 15, beginning with Section 551.

Venue
Petition to be filed in the county in which either party resides. (Sec. 593.)

Grounds
Adultery; imprisonment for three years or more; intolerable severity; willful desertion or absence for seven years; refusal to or neglect of support; incurable insanity; living apart for six months [no-fault divorce]. (Sec. 551.)

Residency
Six months for filing; one year for decree of dissolution to issue. (Sec. 592.)

Property Division
Equitable distribution. Marital misconduct may be considered. All property belonging to either party is marital property subject to division. (Sec. 751.)

Maintenance
Statutory factors are found at Section 752.

Child Custody Enforcement
UCCJA (Sec. 1031.)

Sample Caption
COMPLAINT FOR DIVORCE
VERMONT FAMILY COURT　　　　　_____ COUNTY
DOCKET NUMBER_____

_____　vs.　_____
Plaintiff　　　　　　　　　　Defendant

Virginia

Statute
Code of Virginia beginning with Section 20-89.1.

Venue
Petition to be filed in the county in which the defendant resides, if a resident; otherwise, the county in which the parties last cohabited. (Sec. 8.01-261.)

Grounds
Adultery; imprisonment for one year; cruelty, causing reasonable apprehension of physical harm, or willful desertion once a year has passed after the act; the parties have been living separate and apart for one year [no-fault divorce]; the parties have been living separate and apart for six months, there are no children, and the parties have entered a separation agreement [no-fault divorce]. (Sec. 20-91.)

Residency
Six months. (Sec. 20-97.)

Property Division
Equitable distribution. Property acquired prior to marriage, or by gift or inheritance, is not subject to division. (Sec. 20-107.3.)

Maintenance
No maintenance may be awarded to a party who has committed adultery. (Sec. 107.1.)

Child Custody Enforcement
UCCJEA (Sec. 20-146.1.)

Sample Caption
VIRGINIA: IN THE CIRCUIT COURT OF _____ COUNTY

_____,
Plaintiff,
v.   Civil Action No. _____

_____,
Defendant.

COMPLAINT FOR DIVORCE

Washington

Statute
Revised Code of Washington beginning with Section 26.09.002.

Venue
Petition to be filed in the county in which petitioner resides. (Sec. 26.09.010.)

Grounds
Irretrievable breakdown of marriage [no-fault divorce]. (Sec. 26.09.030.)

Residency
None for filing; ninety days for decree of dissolution. (Sec. 26.09.030.)

Property Division
Community property. Property acquired prior to marriage or by gift or inheritance is not subject to division. (Sec. 26.16.010; 26.16.020.)

Maintenance
Marital misconduct is not a factor. (Sec. 26.09.090.)

Child Custody Enforcement
UCCJA (beginning with Sec. 26.27.011.)

Sample Caption
SUPERIOR COURT OF WASHINGTON
COUNTY OF _____

IN RE THE MARRIAGE OF

_____,   No. _____

Petitioner,
and   PETITION FOR DISSOLUTION

_____,   OF MARRIAGE

Respondent.

West Virginia

Statute
West Virginia Code beginning with Section 48-1-101.

Venue
If respondent is a resident, petition to be filed in the county in which the parties last cohabited or in the county where the respondent resides; otherwise, in the county in which the parties last cohabited or in the county where the petitioner resides. (Sec. 48-5-106.)

Grounds
Irreconcilable differences [no-fault divorce] (Sec. 48-5-201); parties have lived separate and apart for one year [no-fault divorce] (Sec. 48-5-202); cruel or inhuman treatment (Sec. 48-5-203); adultery (Sec. 48-5-204); conviction of a felony (Sec. 48-5-205); permanent and incurable insanity (Sec. 48-5-206); habitual drunkenness or drug addiction (Sec. 48-5-207); desertion for six months (Sec. 48-5-208); abuse of a party or a child of the party (Sec. 48-5-209).

Residency
No time limit if the marriage was entered into in the state and one party remains a resident; otherwise, one year. (Sec. 48-5-105.)

Property Division
Equitable distribution. (Sec. 48-7-101.) Fault is not considered. (Sec. 48-7-103.)

Maintenance
Fault is a factor. (Sec. 48-5-202.) Statutory factors are found at Section 48-6-301.

Child Custody Enforcement
UCCJEA (Sec. 48-20-101.)

Sample Caption
IN THE FAMILY COURT OF _____ COUNTY, WEST VIRGINIA

IN RE THE MARRIAGE OF: CIVIL ACTION NO. _____

_____ and _____
Petitioner,   Respondent.

PETITION FOR DIVORCE

Wisconsin

Statute
Wisconsin Statutes beginning with Section 767.001.

Venue
Petition to be filed in the county in which respondent resides. (Sec. 801.50.)

Grounds
Irretrievable breakdown of the marriage [no-fault divorce]. (Sec. 767.315.)

Residency
Six months. (Sec. 767.301.)

Property Division
Community property. Property acquired prior to marriage, or by gift or inheritance, is not subject to division. (Sec. 767.61.)

Maintenance
Statutory factors are found at Section 767.56.

Child Custody Enforcement
UCCJEA (beginning with Sec. 822.01.)

Sample Caption
STATE OF WISCONSIN, CIRCUIT COURT, _____ COUNTY

In re the Marriage of:

_____,   Petition Case No. _____

Petitioner,

and

_____,

Defendant.

Wyoming

Statute
Wyoming Statutes beginning with Section 20-2-101.

Venue
Petition to be filed in the county in which either party resides. (Sec. 20-2-104.)

Grounds
Irreconcilable differences [no-fault divorce] (Sec. 20-3-104); insanity. (Sec. 20-2-105.)

Residency
Sixty days. (Sec. 20-2-107.)

Property Division
Equitable distribution. (Sec. 20-2-114.)

Maintenance
No statutory factors other than the obligor spouse's ability to pay. (Sec. 20-2-114.)

Child Custody Enforcement
UCCJEA (Sec. 20-5-201.)

Sample Caption

COMPLAINT FOR DIVORCE
IN THE DISTRICT COURT IN AND FOR
_____COUNTY, WYOMING

In Re: The Marriage of   )   _____
)   Civil Action Case No.:
)
_____,   )
Plaintiff,   )
vs.   )
)
_____,   )
Defendant.   )

APPENDIX C:
Sample, Filled-in Forms

This appendix contains filled-in sample forms so you can see how the forms should be filled out. Please visit **www.sphinxlegal.com/extras/quickiedivorce** for blank versions of each form, which you can dowload and fill in with your specific information.

TABLE OF FORMS

IN THE DISTRICT COURT OF THE <u>FIRST</u> JUDICIAL DISTRICT STATE OF <u>EAST DAKOTA</u>

In Re the Marriage of:)
)
<u> Samuel Spouse   </u>   )
                    Petitioner,   )
) CASE NO. <u>2007D1234</u>
and   )
)
<u> Susan Spouse   </u>   )
                    Respondent.   )

PETITION FOR DISSOLUTION OF MARRIAGE

<u>   Samuel Spouse   </u> (name), Petitioner in the above-named case, being duly sworn, states as follows:

1. Petitioner's Information

Petitioner's birthdate is <u>   6/21/1960   </u>.
Petitioner's age is <u>   46   </u>.
Petitioner's Social Security number is <u> 234-56-7890   </u>.
Petitioner's current address is <u>123 Main St., Springfield, ED 60500</u>
Length of residency at this address is <u> 5 years </u>.
If residency is less than 2 years, Petitioner's last address was

<u>   </u>.

Petitioner ___ is <u> x </u> is not (check one) a member of the military.
Petitioner's occupation is <u>   Accountant   </u>.

2. Respondent's Information

Respondent's birthdate is <u>   7/10/1960   </u>.
Respondent's age is <u> 46   </u>.
Respondent's Social Security number is <u> 345-67-8901 </u>.
Respondent's current address is <u> 987 First St., Springfield, ED 60500 </u>.
Length of residency at this address is <u>   3 months   </u>.
If residency is less than 2 years or if Petitioner's address is unknown,

Petitioner's last known address was 123 Main St., Springfield, ED .
Respondent ___is _x_is not (check one) a member of the military.
Respondent's occupation is homemaker   .

3. Marriage

Petitioner and Respondent were married on   November 1, 1988
at   Dakota City, East Dakota   . Petitioner and
Respondent separated on   March 1, 2007   .

4. Children

A completed Uniform Child Custody Jurisdiction and Enforcement Act (UCCJEA) Affidavit must be attached to this petition if Petitioner and Respondent have any dependent minor children together.

a. (check any that apply)

___Petitioner and Respondent have no children together. *If this option is checked, skip section 4.b.*

___Petitioner is pregnant with a due date of _____.

___Respondent is pregnant with a due date of _____.

b. Children of the Marriage Dependent Upon Both Spouses
The husband and wife are both the parents of the following dependent children:

Name (first/last) Sarah Spouse   DOB 2/3/96   Age 11
Name (first/last) Sean Spouse   DOB 5/11/00   Age 6
Name (first/last) _____   DOB _____   Age _____
Name (first/last) _____   DOB _____   Age _____

The husband is and the wife is not the parent of the following dependent children:

Name (first/last) _____   DOB _____   Age _____
Name (first/last) _____   DOB _____   Age _____

The wife is and the husband is not the parent of the following dependent children:

Name (first/last) _____   DOB _____   Age _____
Name (first/last) _____   DOB _____   Age _____

5. Grounds

This marriage should be dissolved because (state grounds for dissolution) _it is irretrievably broken_ .

6. Other Proceedings

(check only one)

_x_ There is no Petition for Dissolution between the parties pending in any other Court.

___There is a Petition for Dissolution pending between the parties in

_____.

(city, county, and state)

7. Marital Property

(check only one)

___There is neither community or separate property owned nor marital debts owed by the parties.

_x_ There is community or separate property owned and/or marital debts owed by the parties. The court should make a fair and equitable division of all the property and debt.

(check all that apply)

___Property and debt should be divided according to written agreement between the parties, a copy of which agreement is attached to the Petition herein.

___The division of property and debt should be determined by the court at a later date.

_x_ Petitioner's recommendation for the division of property and debt is set forth below:

Petitioner should be awarded the parties' interest in the following property: Residence at 123 Main Street, Springfield; all furnishings, books, recordings, decorative items and electronics in the residence as of the date of filing; 2004 minivan; savings in Main Bank savings account #99999001 as of date of filing.

Respondent should be awarded the parties' interest in the following property: 1999 station wagon; furnishings, books and recordings in Respondent's possession as of date of filing

The parties' marital debt should be allocated between the parties as follows:
 Petitioner to assume outstanding mortgage on residence at 123 Main Street, Springfield, ED.

8. Maintenance
(check one only)

 x Spousal maintenance should not be ordered.

____Spousal maintenance should be ordered as follows:

_____
_____
_____

9. Child Custody *If the parties have no dependent children, skip section 9.*
Have the parties agreed to child custody and/or visitation in a written agreement? (check one) ____Yes x No *If Yes, attach written agreement to Petition; if no, complete sections 9.a., 9.b., and 9.c. below.*

a. Legal custody (check only one)

 x It is in the child(ren)'s best interest that legal custody be shared by both parties.

____It is in the child(ren)'s best interest that legal custody be awarded solely to (check one) ____Petitioner ____Respondent, because

_____
_____.

b. Physical custody (check only one)

 x It is in the child(ren)'s best interest that physical custody be shared by both parties.

____It is in the child(ren)'s best interest that physical custody be awarded solely to (check one)____Petitioner ____Respondent, because

_____
_____.

c. Visitation (check only one)

___It is in the child(ren)'s best interest that the Court provide for parental visitation as follows:

_____

___It is in the child(ren)'s best interest that the Court (check one)
___deny
___restrict visitation, because_____

_____

10. Child Support *If the parties have no dependent children, skip section 10.* (check all that apply)

_x_ Petitioner requests the Court award child support pursuant to the State of East Dakota Child Support Guidelines, with such support retroactive to <u>March 1, 2001</u> (date).

___Petitioner requests that the Court order support to be paid beyond the age of 18 years because

_____

_____

___Petitioner requests that the Court award child support in an amount that is more or less than the State of East Dakota Child Support Guidelines, because

_____

___Petitioner requests that (check only one) _x_ Petitioner ___ Respondent be ordered to provide medical and dental insurance coverage for the dependent minor child(ren).

___Petitioner requests that (check only one) ___Petitioner ___Respondent _x_ both be ordered to pay all uninsured medical and dental expenses for the dependent minor child(ren).

___Petitioner requests that life insurance to secure child support be provided by (check only one) ___Petitioner ___Respondent _x_ both.

Relief Requested

The Petitioner respectfully requests the Court to enter a Decree of Dissolution of Marriage, and to grant the following relief (check all that apply):

1. distribute marital property and debt as requested in section 7 of the Petition;
2. grant spousal maintenance as requested in section 8 of the Petition;

award child custody and visitation as requested in section 9 of the Petition; grant child support for the dependent minor child(ren) of both parties as requested in section 10 of the Petition; and for such other relief as this Honorable Court deems necessary and proper.

Dated: _____ 4/1/07 _____   *Samuel Spouse* _____
                                   Signature of Petitioner

                                   Samuel Spouse _____
                                   Print or Type Name

I declare under penalty of perjury under the laws of the State of East Dakota that the foregoing is true and correct.
Signed at Springfield, [City] East Dakota [State] on April 1, 2007 [Date].

*Samuel Spouse* _____   Samuel Spouse _____
Signature of Petitioner   Print or Type Name

SWORN TO AND subscribed before me in the County of Springfield, on April 1 _____, 2007 .

Nancy Notary _____
NOTARY PUBLIC

My Commission Expires: notary seal
June 1, 2007

IN THE DISTRICT COURT OF THE <u>FIRST</u> JUDICIAL DISTRICT STATE OF <u>EAST DAKOTA</u>

In Re the Marriage of:)
)
  <u>Samuel Spouse</u>   )
                      Petitioner,   )
)   CASE NO. <u>2007D1234</u>
and   )
)
  <u>Susan Spouse</u>   )
                      Respondent.   )

SIMPLIFIED PETITION FOR DISSOLUTION OF MARRIAGE

NOW COME <u>Samuel Spouse</u>, Petitioner, and <u>Susan Spouse</u>, Respondent, both pro se, and hereby petition this Honorable Court for dissolution of the marriage between Petitioner and Respondent. In support of this Petition, the parties state as follows:

1. Petitioner resides in <u>Dakota County, East Dakota</u>, and has lived there since <u>November, 2001</u>. Respondent resides in <u>Dakota County, East Dakota</u>, and has lived there since <u>November, 2001</u>.

Petitioner and Respondent were married <u>November 1, 1988</u>, in the town of <u>Dakota City, East Dakota</u>.

The marriage of Petitioner and Respondent is irretrievably broken.

Petitioner and Respondent have no minor dependent children and <u>Respondent</u> is not now pregnant.

Petitioner and Respondent have entered into a marital settlement agreement dividing their assets and liabilities, and have filed with this Petition signed Financial Affidavits.

Neither Petitioner nor Respondent were pressured or forced into signing this Petition.

WHEREFORE, Petitioner and Respondent respectfully request that this Honorable Court approve the marital settlement agreement and enter its order of Dissolution of Marriage.

Respectfully,

<u>*Samuel Spouse*</u>
Petitioner

Dated: <u>April 1, 2007</u>   <u>*Samuel Spouse*</u>
Signature of Petitioner

<u>Samuel Spouse</u>
Print or Type Name

I declare under penalty of perjury under the laws of the State of <u>East Dakota</u> that the foregoing is true and correct.

Signed at <u>Dakota City, East Dakota</u>, on <u>April 1, 2007</u>.

<u>*Samuel Spouse*</u>   <u>Samuel Spouse</u>
Signature of Petitioner   Print or Type Name

SWORN TO AND subscribed before me in the County of <u>Dakota</u> _____, on <u>April 1</u>_____, 2007.

<u>*Nancy Notary*</u>
NOTARY PUBLIC
My Commission Expires: notary seal
November 1, 2007

Dated: <u>April 1, 2007</u>   <u>*Susan Spouse*</u>
Signature of Respondent

<u>Susan Spouse</u>
Print or Type Name

IN THE DISTRICT COURT OF THE <u>FIRST</u> JUDICIAL DISTRICT
STATE OF <u>EAST DAKOTA</u>

In Re the Marriage of:)
)
<u> Samuel Spouse   </u>   )
             Petitioner,   )
)   CASE NO. <u>2007D1234</u>
)
and   )
)
<u> Susan Spouse   </u>)
             Respondent.)

SUMMONS

To each Respondent:

You are summoned and required to file an answer to the Petition in this case, a copy of which is hereto attached, or otherwise file your appearance in the office of the Clerk of this Court, <u>364 Sycamore Street, Springfield, East Dakota,</u> within 30 days after service of this summons, not counting the day of service. IF YOU FAIL TO DO SO, A JUDGMENT BY DEFAULT MAY BE TAKEN AGAINST YOU FOR THE RELIEF REQUESTED IN THE PETITION.

To the Officer:

This summons must be returned by the Officer or other person to whom it was given for service, with the endorsement of service and fees, if any, immediately after service. If service cannot be made, this summons shall be returned so endorsed. THIS SUMMONS MAY NOT BE SERVED LATER THAN 30 DAYS AFTER ITS DATE.

(seal of court)   WITNESS: <u>Joseph Crow</u>, Clerk of the
                            <u>First</u> Judicial District

DATED: <u>April 1, 2007</u>
George Repp
Petitioner's Attorney (or Petitioner, if not represented by attorney)

Clerk of the First Judicial District
<u>364 Sycamore Street</u>   DATE OF SERVICE: <u>April 14, 2007</u>
<u>Springfield, East Dakota</u>   (to be inserted by officer on copy
<u>(101) 555-6677</u>   left with defendant or other person)

IN THE DISTRICT COURT OF THE <u>FIRST</u> JUDICIAL DISTRICT STATE OF <u>EAST DAKOTA</u>

In Re the Marriage of:)
)
<u> Samuel Spouse   </u>)
               Petitioner,)
)   CASE NO. <u>2007D1234</u>
and   )
)
<u> Susan Spouse   </u>)
              Respondent.)

APPEARANCE

I HEREBY ENTER THE APPEARANCE OF <u> Samuel Spouse   </u>
                    (name of party for whom appearance is entered)

AND MY OWN AS

<u> X </u> REGULAR COUNSEL   ___ TRIAL COUNSEL
___ SPECIAL APPEARANCE   ___ SUBSTITUTE COUNSEL
___ PRO SE   ___ COUNSEL IN FORCIBLE
                                     ENTRY

___ ADDITIONAL COUNSEL   ___ APPELLATE COUNSEL
___ GUARDIAN AD LITEM   ___ COURT APPOINTED
                                     COUNSEL

AND AS HIS COUNSEL IN THE ABOVE ENTITLED CASE.

                            SIGNED<u>   **George Repp**   </u>
                                  (signature of attorney)

Name <u> George Repp   </u>
Attorney for <u>Petitioner   </u>
Address <u> 567 Business Drive   </u>
City, State, Zip <u>Springfield, ED   </u>
Phone <u>(101) 555-4567   </u>

IN THE DISTRICT COURT OF THE <u>FIRST</u> JUDICIAL DISTRICT STATE OF <u>EAST DAKOTA</u>

In Re the Marriage of:)
)
<u> Samuel Spouse   </u>)
             Petitioner,)
)   CASE NO. <u>2007D1234</u>
)
and)
)
<u> Susan Spouse   </u>)
            Respondent.)

RESPONSE TO PETITION FOR DISSOLUTION

NOW COMES the Respondent, <u>Susan Spouse</u>, by her attorney, <u>Lawrence Lawyer</u>, and in Response to Petitioner's Petition for Dissolution of Marriage, states as follows:

1. Respondent <u>ADMITS</u> the allegations of paragraph 1 of Petitioner's Petition for Dissolution.
2. Respondent <u>ADMITS</u> the allegations of paragraph 2 Petitioner's Petition for Dissolution.
3. Respondent <u>ADMITS</u> the allegations of paragraph 3 of Petitioner's Petition for Dissolution.
4. Respondent <u>ADMITS</u> the allegations of paragraph 4 of Petitioner's Petition for Dissolution.
5. Respondent <u>ADMITS</u> the allegations of paragraph 5 of Petitioner's Petition for Dissolution.
6. Respondent <u>ADMITS</u> the allegations of paragraph 6 of Petitioner's Petition for Dissolution.
7. Respondent <u>ADMITS</u> the allegations of paragraph 7 of Petitioner's Petition for Dissolution <u>regarding the existence of marital property, but DENIES that Petitioner should be granted the marital residence.</u>

Respondent further states that the marital home should be granted to Respondent.

8. Respondent <u>DENIES</u> the allegations of paragraph 8 of Petitioner's Petition for Dissolution <u>that spousal support should not be ordered, and affirmatively states that Petitioner should be ordered to provide rehabilitative spousal support in an amount and for a duration that the Court deems necessary for Respondent to update her skills to a level that she might have attained had she not previously ended her career for Petitioner's benefit during the marriage.</u>

9. Respondent <u>DENIES</u> the allegations of paragraph 9 of Petitioner's Petition for Dissolution <u>that child custody should be shared by both Respondent and Petitioner, and affirmatively states that Respondent should be granted sole legal and physical custody of the children, because Respondent has been the primary parent for the children for their entire lives, the children's preference is that Respondent remain the primary parent, and Respondent is more likely to facilitate a relationship between the children and Petitioner.</u>

10. Respondent <u>DENIES</u> the allegations of paragraph 10 of Petitioner's Petition for Dissolution, <u>and affirmatively states as follows:</u>

a. <u>that the Court should order Petitioner to pay child support in excess of State of East Dakota guidelines, in view of Petitioner's insistence that the children attend parochial school;</u>

b. <u>that the Court should order Petitioner to pay child support for each child beyond the age of 18 years, in view of Petitioner's insistence that the children attend private college;</u>

c. <u>that the Court should order Petitioner to pay for all medical and dental insurance coverage as well as uninsured medical and dental expenses for the children; and,</u>

d. <u>that the Court should require Petitioner to maintain a life insurance policy for himself in a benefit amount sufficient to cover all above expenses in the event of Petitioner's death.</u>

Relief Requested

The Respondent respectfully requests the Court to enter a Decree of Dissolution of Marriage, and to grant the following relief:

1. distribute marital property and debt as requested in section 7 of the Petition;

2. grant spousal maintenance to Respondent as requested in section 8 of the Petition;

3 award child custody and visitation to Respondent as requested in section 9 of the Petition;

4. grant child support to Respondent for the dependent minor child(ren) of both parties as requested in section 10 of the Petition;

5. and for such other relief as this Honorable Court deems necessary and proper.

Dated: May 1, 2007   _Susan Spouse_____
                       Signature of Petitioner

                       Susan Spouse_____
                       Print or Type Name

I declare under penalty of perjury under the laws of the State of East Dakota that the foregoing is true and correct.

Signed at Dakota City, ED on May 1, 2007.

___Susan Spouse_____   _____Susan Spouse_____

SWORN TO AND subscribed before me in the County of Dakota, on May 1, 2007.

_____Nancy Notary_____
NOTARY PUBLIC
My Commission Expires:
November 1, 2007   notary seal

IN THE DISTRICT COURT OF THE <u>FIRST</u> JUDICIAL DISTRICT STATE OF <u>EAST DAKOTA</u>

In Re the Marriage of:)
)
<u> Samuel Spouse </u>   )
                    Petitioner,   )
)   CASE NO. <u>2007D1234</u>
and   )
)
<u> Susan Spouse </u>   )
                    Respondent.   )

FINANCIAL AFFIDAVIT

<u>Samuel Spouse</u>, Petitioner in the above-captioned case, having been duly sworn, hereby states the following for his Financial Affidavit:

PERSONAL DATA
FULL NAME   <u>   Samuel Steven Spouse   </u>

DATE OF BIRTH   <u>   6/21/60   </u>

RESIDENTIAL ADDRESS<u>   123 Main Street   </u>
<u>   Springfield, ED 60500   </u>

EMPLOYER   <u>   T and G Rock Accountants   </u>
EMPLOYER'S ADDRESS <u>201 Third Street, Springfield, ED   </u>

NUMBER OF DEPENDENTS CLAIMED <u>   2   </u>

PAY PERIOD (WEEKLY, ETC.)   <u>   monthly   </u>

RENT OR OWN RESIDENCE?   <u>   own   </u>

INCOME
GROSS MONTHLY INCOME   <u> $6,000.00   </u>   FROM
EMPLOYMENT (SALARY OR WAGES)

CHILD SUPPORT CURRENTLY<u> $0   </u>   BEING RECEIVED

INTEREST, DIVIDEND_____ $0
OR OTHER INVESTMENT INCOME

UNEMPLOYMENT, WORKERS' _____ $0
COMPENSATION, DISABILITY INCOME

OTHER INCOME _____ $0
(SPECIFY SOURCES AND AMOUNTS) _____ n/a
_____ n/a

TOTAL GROSS MONTHLY INCOME
   $6,000.00_____

LIQUID ASSETS/ASSET VALUE

SAVINGS AND CHECKING _____ $4,500.00
ACCOUNTS

CERTIFICATES OF DEPOSIT _____ $0

MONEY MARKET ACCOUNTS _____ $0

STOCK OR BOND _____ $0
INSTRUMENTS

OTHER CASH ON HAND _____ n/a
OR CASH EQUIVALENT

TOTAL LIQUID ASSETS _____ $4,500.00

MANDATORY MONTHLY DEDUCTIONS FROM INCOME

FEDERAL TAX _____ $1,500.00

STATE TAX _____ $350.00

FICA _____ $50.00

UNION DUES _____ $0

HEALTH INSURANCE _____ $100.00
PREMIUMS REQUIRED BY EMPLOYER

DEDUCTIONS REQUIRED BY _____ n/a
COURT ORDER
MISCELLANEOUS REQUIRED _____ n/a
DEDUCTIONS

TOTAL MONTHLY _____ $2,000.00
DEDUCTIONS

MONTHLY EXPENSES

RENT OR MORTGAGE _____ $1,400.00

PROPERTY TAXES _____ n/a

INSURANCE (MORTGAGE, _____ n/a
RENTER'S, HOMEOWNER'S, ETC.)

UTILITIES (WATER/SEWER, _____ $300.00
GAS, ELECTRIC, CABLE OR SATELLITE, TELEPHONE, GARBAGE
REMOVAL, ETC.)

FOOD AND SUNDRIES _____ $200.00
(INCLUDE RESTAURANT MEALS, PERSONAL HYGIENE ITEMS,
OFFICE/SCHOOL SUPPLIES, PET CARE, ETC.)

CLOTHING (PURCHASE _____ $500.00
AND CLEANING FOR ALL HOUSEHOLD MEMBERS)

HEALTH CARE (INCLUDE _____ $100.00
MEDICAL AND DENTAL EXPENSES AND INSURANCE FOR ALL
HOUSEHOLD MEMBERS

TRANSPORTATION _____ $300.00
(INCLUDE CAR LOAN PAYMENTS, AUTO INSURANCE OF ANY
TYPE, GASOLINE, MAINTENANCE/REPAIR, MASS TRANSIT
EXPENSES, PARKING AND OTHER EXPENSES)
CHILDREN (INCLUDE TUITION, _____ $300.00

EXTRACURRICULAR ACTIVITIES, DAY CARE, BABYSITTING, ANY
OTHER CHILD-RELATED EXPENSES NOT PREVIOUSLY STATED)

RECREATION (INCLUDE _____ $500.00 _____
HOBBIES, BOOKS/MAGAZINES, VACATIONS, OTHER ENTERTAIN-
MENT)

DEBT PAYMENTS (INCLUDE_____ n/a _____
PRIOR COURT-ORDERED CHILD SUPPORT PAYMENTS, CREDIT
CARD BALANCES, AND OTHER DEBT NOT PREVIOUSLY STATED)

MISCELLANEOUS EXPENSES_____ $0 _____
(SPECIFY TYPE AND AMOUNT)
_____ n/a _____

_____ n/a _____

TOTAL MONTHLY EXPENSES
_____ $3,600.00 ____

The undersigned states under oath, under penalties for perjury, that this
Financial Affidavit includes all of his income and expenses, he has knowledge of the matters stated, and he certifies that the statements set forth
herein are true and correct, except as to matters stated to be on information
and belief, and as to such matters the undersigned certifies as aforesaid that
he believes the same to be true.

_**Samuel Spouse**_____
Affiant

SWORN TO AND subscribed before me in the County of <u>Dakota</u>, on
<u>April 15, 2007</u>.

_____*Nancy Notary*_____
NOTARY PUBLIC
My Commission Expires: notary seal
<u>November 1, 2007</u>

IN THE DISTRICT COURT OF THE <u>FIRST</u> JUDICIAL DISTRICT STATE OF <u>EAST DAKOTA</u>

In Re the Marriage of:)
)
<u>　Samuel Spouse　　　　　</u>)
　　　　　　　Petitioner,)
)　　CASE <u>NO.2007D1234</u>
and)
)
<u>　Susan Spouse　　　　　　</u>)
　　　　　　Respondent.)

UCCJEA AFFIDAVIT

<u>Samuel Spouse　　　　　</u>, Petitioner herein, being duly sworn, deposes and states as follows:

1. Petitioner resides at <u>123 Main Street, Springfield, East Dakota</u>.

2. Upon information and belief, the children who are subject to this proceeding currently reside at:

Name	Date of Birth	Address
<u>Sarah Spouse</u>	<u>2/3/96</u>	<u>123 Main Street, Springfield, ED</u>
<u>Sean Spouse</u>	<u>5/11/00</u>	<u>123 Main Street, Springfield, ED</u>

3. Upon information and belief, the children who are subject to this proceeding have, during the previous five years, have resided at the following:

Name	Address	Dates of Residence
<u>Sarah Spouse</u>	<u>123 Main Street,</u> <u>Springfield</u>	<u>11/1/01-present</u>
<u>Sean Spouse</u>	<u>123 Main Street,</u> <u>Springfield</u>	<u>11/1/01-present</u>

4. Upon information and belief, the children who are subject to this proceeding have, during the previous five years, resided with the following persons:

Name	Address	Dates of Residence
<u>Samuel Spouse</u>	<u>123 Main Street,</u> <u>Springfield</u>	<u>4/1/02-present</u>

| Susan Spouse | 123 Main Street, Springfield | 4/1/02-present |

5. Petitioner ___Samuel Spouse ~~has~~/has not participated as a party/witness/other _____ (indicate capacity) in other litigation concerning the custody of the same children in this or any other state.

6. Petitioner _Samuel Spouse_ ~~has~~/has not information of any custody proceeding concerning the child pending in a court of this or any other state.

7. Petitioner _Samuel Spouse_ ~~knows~~/does not know of any person not a party to the proceedings who has physical custody of the child or claims to have custody or visitation rights with respect to the children.

If the declarations in either paragraph 5, 6, or 7 are in the affirmative, Petitioner shall provide additional information to the Court under oath. Petitioner understands that he has a continuing duty to inform the Court of any custody proceeding concerning the child in this or any other state of which she obtained information during this proceeding.

STATE OF _EAST DAKOTA_)
)
COUNTY OF _SPRINGFIELD_)

Samuel Spouse, being first duly sworn on oath, deposes and states that he/she has read the foregoing document, and the answers made herein are true, correct and complete to the best of her knowledge and belief.

Samuel Spouse
SIGNATURE

SUBSCRIBED and SWORN to before me this _1st_ day of _April_, 2007.

Nancy Notary
NOTARY PUBLIC   notary seal

MY COMMISSION EXPIRES:
November 1, 2007

IN THE DISTRICT COURT OF THE <u>FIRST</u> JUDICIAL DISTRICT
STATE OF <u>EAST DAKOTA</u>

In Re the Marriage of:)
)
<u> Samuel Spouse   </u>   )
                       Petitioner,   )
)   CASE NO. <u>2007D1234</u>
and   )
)
<u> Susan Spouse   </u>   )
                       Respondent.   )

INTERROGATORIES

1. State your full name, current address, date of birth and the last four
   digits of your Social Security number.
   <u>Samuel Steven Spouse 123 Main Street, Springfield, ED</u>
   <u>6/21/60</u>
   <u>8901</u>
2. List all employment held by you during the preceding three years and
   with regard to each employment state:
   a. The name and address of each employer;
      <u>T and G Rock Accountants, 201 Third St., Springfield, ED</u>
   b. Your position, job title or description;
      <u>Staff Accountant</u>
      If you had an employment contract;
      <u>No</u>
   d. The date on which you commenced your employment and, if appli-
      cable, the date and reason for the termination of your employment;
      <u>Commenced 1/2/97</u>
   e. Your current gross and net income per pay period;
      Gross: <u>$6,000.00/mo.</u>; Net: <u>$4,000.00/mo.</u>
   f. Your gross income as shown on the last W-2 tax and wage statement
      received by you, your Social Security wages as shown on the last W-2
      tax and wage statement received by you, and the amounts of all deduc-
      tions shown thereon; and
      <u>$72,000 gross annual income</u>

g. All additional benefits or perquisites received from your employment stating the type and value thereof. <u>NA</u>

3. During the preceding three years, have you had any source of income other than from your employment listed above? If so, with regard to each source of income, state the following: <u>No</u>
   a. The source of income, including the type of income and name and address of the source;
   b. The frequency in which you receive income from the source;
   c. The amount of income received by you from the source during the immediately preceding three years; and
   d. The amount of income received by you from the source for each month during the immediately preceding three years.

4. Do you own any interest in real estate? If so, with regard to each such interest state the following: <u>No</u>
   a. The size and description of the parcel of real estate, including improvements thereon;
   b. The name, address, and interest of each person who has or claims to have an ownership interest in the parcel of real estate;
   c. The date your interest in the parcel of real estate was acquired;
   d. The consideration you transferred or paid for your interest in the parcel of real estate;
   e. Your estimate of the current fair market value of the parcel of real estate and your interest therein; and,
   f. The amount of any indebtedness owed on the parcel of real estate and to whom.

5. For the preceding three years, list the names and addresses of all associations, partnerships, corporations, enterprises, or entities in which you have an interest or claim any interest; the nature of your interest or claim of interest therein; the amount of percentage of your interest or claim of interest therein; and an estimate of the value of your interest therein. <u>NA</u>

6. During the preceding three years, have you had any account or investment in any type of financial institution, individually or with another or in the name of another, including checking accounts, savings accounts, certificates of deposit, and money market accounts? If so, with regard to each such account or investment, state the following:
   a. The type of account or investment;
      <u>checking account</u>
   b. The name and address of the financial institution;
      <u>Main Bank, Springfield, ED</u>
   c. The name and address of each person in whose name the account is held;
      <u>Samuel Spouse</u>
      <u>123 Main St.</u>
      <u>Springfield, ED</u>
      and
   d. Both the high and the low balance of the account or investment, stating the date of the high balance and the date of the low balance.
      <u>$2,000.00 on 6/9/01</u>
      <u>$5,000.00 on 5/3/03</u>

7. During the preceding three years, have you been the holder of or had access to any safety deposit boxes? If so, state the following: <u>No</u>
   a. The name of the bank or institution where such box is located;
   b. The number of each box;
   c. A description of the contents of each box during the immediately preceding three years and as of the date of the answer; and,
   d. The name and address of any joint or co-owners of such safety deposit box or any trustees holding the box for your benefit.

8. During the immediately preceding three years, has any person or entity held cash or property on your behalf? If so, state: <u>No</u>
   a. The name and address of the person or entity holding the cash or property; and
   b. The type of cash or property held and the value thereof.

9. During the preceding three years, have you owned any stocks, bonds, securities or other investments, including savings bonds? If so, with regard to each such stock, bond, security or investment state: <u>No</u>

a. A description of the stock, bond, security or investment;
b. The name and address of the entity issuing the stock, bond, security or investment;
c. The present value of such stock, bond, security or investment;
d. The date of acquisition of the stock, bond, security or investment;
e. The cost of the stock, bond, security or investment;
f. The name and address of any other owner or owners in such stock, bond, security or investment; and,
g. If applicable, the date sold and the amount realized therefrom.

10. Do you own or have any incidents of ownership in any life, annuity, or endowment insurance policies? If so, with regard to each such policy state: <u>No</u>
a. The name of the company;
b. The number of the policy;
c. The face value of the policy;
d. The present value of the policy;
e. The amount of any loan or encumbrance on the policy;
f. The date of acquisition of the policy; and,
g. With regard to each policy, the beneficiary or beneficiaries.

11. Do you have any right, title, claim, or interest in or to a pension plan, retirement plan, or profit sharing plan, including, but not limited to, individual retirement accounts, 401(k) plans, and deferred compensation plans? If so, with regard to each such plan state: <u>Yes</u>
The name and address of the entity providing the plan;
<u>E-Z Retirement, Inc.</u>
<u>200 Fourth Street</u>
<u>Anytown, ED</u>
The date of your initial participation in the plan; and
<u>1/2/97</u>
The amount of funds currently held on your behalf under the plan.
<u>$35,015.02</u>

12. Do you have any outstanding indebtedness or financial obligations, including mortgages, promissory notes, or other oral or written contracts? If so, with regard to each obligation state the following: <u>No</u>

a. The name and address of the creditor;
b. The form of the obligation;
c. The date the obligation was initially incurred;
d. The amount of the original obligation;
e. The purpose or consideration for which the obligation was incurred;
f. A description of any security connected with the obligation;
g. The rate of interest on the obligation;
h. The present unpaid balance of the obligation;
i. The dates and amounts of installment payments; and,
j. The date of maturity of the obligation.

13. Are you owed any money or property? If so, state: <u>No</u>
a. The name and address of the debtor;
b. The form of the obligation;
c. The date the obligation was initially incurred;
d. The amount of the original obligation;
e. The purpose or consideration for which the obligation was incurred;
f. The description of any security connected with the obligation;
g. The rate of interest on the obligation;
h. The present unpaid balance of the obligation;
i. The dates and amounts of installment payments; and,
j. The date of maturity of the obligation.

14. State the year, make, and model of each motor or motorized vehicle, motor or mobile home, and farm machinery or equipment in which you have an ownership, estate, interest, or claim of interest, whether individually or with another, and with regard to each item state:
   <u>2004 Tohondishi Minivan</u>
The date the item was acquired;
   <u>10/1/03</u>
The consideration paid for the item;
   <u>$30,000</u>
The name and address of each other person who has a right, title, claim, or interest in or to the item;
   <u>Sam Spouse, 123 Main St., Springfield, ED</u>
   <u>Susan Spouse, 987 First St., Springfield, ED</u>
The approximate fair market value of the item; and,
   <u>$22,000</u>

The amount of any indebtedness on the item and the name and address of the creditor.
    <u>none</u>

15. Have you purchased or contributed toward the payment for or provided other consideration or improvement with regard to any real estate, motorized vehicle, financial account or securities, or other property, real or personal, on behalf of another person or entity other than your spouse during the preceding three years. If so, with regard to each such transaction state: <u>No</u>
   a. The name and address of the person or entity to whom you contributed;
   b. The type of contribution made by you;
   c. The type of property to which the contribution was made;
   d. The location of the property to which the contribution was made;
   e. Whether or not there is written evidence of the existence of a loan; and,
   f. A description of the written evidence.

16. During the preceding three years, have you made any gift of cash or property, real or personal, to any person or entity not your spouse? If so, with regard to each such transaction state: <u>No</u>
   a. A description of the gift;
   b. The value of the gift;
   c. The date of the gift;
   d. The name and address of the person or entity receiving the gift;
   e. Whether or not there is written evidence of the existence of a gift; and,
   f. A description of the written evidence.

17. During the preceding three years, have you made any loans to any person or entity not your spouse and, if so, with regard to each such loan state: <u>No</u>
   a. A description of the loan;
   b. The value of the loan;
   c. The date of the loan;
   d. The name and address of the person or entity receiving the loan;
   e. Whether or not there is written evidence of the existence of a loan; and,
   f. A description of the written evidence.

18. During the preceding three years, have you sold, transferred, conveyed, encumbered, concealed, damaged, or otherwise disposed of any property owned by you and/or your spouse individually or collectively? If so, with regard to each item of property state: <u>No</u>

   a. A description of the property;

   b. The current location of the property;

   c. The purpose or reason for the action taken by you with regard to the property;

   d. The approximate fair market value of the property;

   e. Whether or not there is written evidence of any such transaction; and,

   f. A description of the written evidence.

19. During the preceding three years, have any appraisals been made with regard to any of the property listed by you under your answers to these interrogatories? If so, state: <u>No</u>

   a. The name and address of the person conducting each such appraisal;

   b. A description of the property appraised;

   c. The date of the appraisal; and,

   d. The location of any copies of each such appraisal.

20. During the preceding three years, have you prepared or has anyone prepared for you any financial statements, net worth statements, or lists of assets and liabilities pertaining to your property or financial affairs? If so, with regard to each such document state: <u>No</u>

   a. The name and address of the person preparing each such document;

   b. The type of document prepared;

   c. The date the document was prepared; and,

   d. The location of all copies of each such document.

21. State the name and address of any accountant, tax preparer, bookkeeper and other person, firm, or entity who has kept or prepared books, documents, and records with regard to your income, property, business, or financial affairs during the course of this marriage. <u>N/A</u>

22. List all nonmarital property claimed by you, identifying each item of property as to the type of property, the date received, the basis on which you claim it is nonmarital property, its location, and the present value of the property.

<u>Limoges china bowl, $4,000, nonmarital property having been
inherited during marriage</u>

23. List all marital property of this marriage, identifying each item of
property as to the type of property, the basis on which you claim it to
be marital property, its location, and the present value of the property.
<u>House, car, savings account, having been acquired during the
marriage and title having been placed in both names</u>

24. What contribution or dissipation has your spouse made to the marital
estate, including but not limited to each of the items or property iden-
tified in response to interrogatories No. 22 and No. 23 above, citing
specifics, if any, for each item of property? <u>unknown</u>

25. Provide the name and address of each witness who will testify at trial
and state the subject of each witness' testimony. <u>none</u>

26. Provide the name and address of each opinion witness who will offer
any testimony, and state: <u>none</u>
   a. The subject matter on which the opinion witness is expected to testify;
   b. The conclusions and/or opinions of the opinion witness and the
      basis c. therefor, including reports of the witness, if any;
   c. The qualifications of each opinion witness, including a curriculum
      vitae and/or resume, if any; and,
   d. The identity of any written reports of the opinion witness regarding
      this occurrence.

27. Are you in any manner incapacitated or limited in your ability to earn
income at the present time? If so, define and describe such incapacity
or limitation, and state when such incapacity or limitation
commenced and when it is expected to end. <u>No</u>

28. Identify any statements, information, and/or documents known to you and
requested by any of the foregoing interrogatories which you claim to be
work product or subject to any common law or statutory privilege, and
with respect to each interrogatory, specify the legal basis for the claim. <u>none</u>

29. List all business, commercial, and professional licenses that you have obtained.
    <u>Certified Public Accountant certification</u>

30. List all of your education including, but not limited to, vocational or specialized training, including the following:
    name and address of each educational institution;
    <u>East Dakota State University</u>
    <u>Dakota City, ED</u>
    dates of attendance; and
    <u>8/78 to 5/82</u>
    degrees of certificates obtained or anticipated dates of same.
    <u>B.S. Accountancy, 5/82</u>

Attestation
STATE OF <u>EAST DAKOTA</u>)
)
COUNTY OF <u>SPRINGFIELD</u>)
<u>Samuel Spouse</u>, being first duly sworn on oath, deposes and states that he is a defendant in the above-captioned matter, that he has read the fore-going document, and the answers made herein are true, correct and complete to the best of his knowledge and belief.

<u>Samuel Spouse</u>
SIGNATURE

SUBSCRIBED and SWORN to before me this
  <u>1st</u> day of <u>May   </u>, <u>2007</u>.

  <u>Nancy Notary</u>   notary seal
NOTARY PUBLIC

MY COMMISSION EXPIRES:
<u>November 1, 2007</u>

IN THE DISTRICT COURT OF THE <u>FIRST</u> JUDICIAL DISTRICT STATE OF <u>EAST DAKOTA</u>

In Re the Marriage of:)
)
<u> Samuel Spouse   </u>   )
              Petitioner,)
)   CASE NO. <u>2007D1234</u>
and   )
)
<u> Susan Spouse   </u>   )
           Respondent.)

REQUEST FOR PRODUCTION

PLEASE TAKE NOTICE that <u>Samuel Spouse</u>, Petitioner herein, demands that the Respondent produce, for inspection and copying, the following documents at the <u>Law Offices of George Repp, 567 Business Drive, Springfield, ED, on June 1, 2007 at 10:00 a.m.</u>:

1. Any and all of your paycheck stubs from all employers for the past <u>36</u> months.

2. Any and all of your monthly retirement account statements from all employers for the past <u>36</u> months.

3. Any and all statements relating to any pension, profit-sharing, employee stock ownership, stock option, or deferred compensation plan owned by you, whether vested or unvested, for the past <u>36</u> months.

4. Any and all documentation relating to any health plan to which you belong, including any and all statements showing premiums paid by you and/or benefits paid to you, whether for your own or any of your dependents' health care for the past <u>36</u> months.

5. If applicable, any and all statements relating to military retirement pay paid or owed to you, for the past <u>36</u> months.

6. Any and all documentation relating to any of the following for which you received any income for the past <u>36</u> months:

      Social Security payments
      Disability payments
      Pension payments
      Dividends
      Patents
      Trademarks
      Copyrights
      Royalties
      Franchises
      Trusts
      Investments
      Rents

7. Any and all documentation relating to any prizes, awards, gifts, rewards, or inheritances, valued at an amount greater than $500, received by you in the past 36 months.

8. Any and all documentation relating to any transfer, including transfer by sale, lease, abandonment, or gift, of any property in which you or your spouse, whether individually, jointly, or with any third party or parties, have or had any interest, which transfer took place at any time in the past 36 months.

9. Any and all documentation relating to any outstanding debts or accounts receivable owed to you or your spouse, whether individually, jointly, or with any third party or parties, for the past 36 months.

10. Statements for any and all checking, savings, credit union, and money market accounts, as well as certificates of deposit, which are held either in your name or your spouse's name, whether individually, jointly, or with any third party or parties, for the past 36 months.

11. Statements for any and all mutual funds, stocks, bonds, other securities, IRA accounts, KEOGH accounts, 401(K) accounts, or other investment funds, which are held either in your name or your spouse's name, whether individually, jointly, or with any third party or parties, for the past 36 months.

12. Any and all state and federal income tax returns, including all schedules, W-2 forms, and other attachments, for the calendar years 2002–2007.

13. Any and all appraisals or assessments for all personal property in which you and/or your spouse own any interest.

14. Any and all deeds, mortgages, promissory notes, tax bills, property tax assessments, appraisals, HUD-1 or other settlement statements, federal income mortgage interest statements for all real property in which you and/or your spouse own any interest or have owned any interest for the past <u>36</u> months.

15. Any and all life insurance policies or documentation reflecting the cash value of any such policies in which you or your spouse have had any interest in the past <u>36</u> months.

16. Any and all of your credit reports or histories you have received in the past <u>36</u> months.

17. Any and all credit card statements for all charge accounts held in your name, whether individually or jointly, for the past <u>36</u> months.

18. Any and all documentation relating to any other indebtedness owed by you as of the date of service of this Request for Production.

19. Any and all state and federal income tax returns for any business, corporation, or partnership in which you are a partner, owner, or shareholder of more than a 5% interest, including all schedules and attachments, for the calendar years <u>2002–2007</u>.

20. Any and all documentation of receipts and disbursements, including accounts receivable and accounts payable ledgers, for any business, corporation, or partnership in which you are a partner, owner, or shareholder of more than a 5% interest, for the calendar years <u>2002–2007</u>.

21. For any business, corporation, or partnership in which you are a partner, owner, or shareholder of more than a 5% interest, any and all of the following documentation:
    Articles of incorporation and by-laws;
    Partnership agreements;
    Loan applications;
    Financial statements;

Appraisals or assessments for all personal property owned by such business entity;

Deeds, mortgages, promissory notes, tax bills, property tax assessments, appraisals, HUD-1 or other settlement statements, federal income mortgage interest statements for all real property owned by such business entity;

Stock certificates;

Shareholder agreements;

Documents relating to your or your spouse's use of or entitlement to use of any business expense account, including but not limited to reimbursement for travel, lodging, or other personal living expenses; and,

Documents relating to your or spouse's use of or entitlement to use of any business loans; life, health, or other insurance; stock ownership, stock options or stock bonuses; profit-sharing, or any other employee benefit plans for any business, corporation, or partnership in which you are a partner, owner, or shareholder of more than a five percent interest.

22. Any and all documentation relating to your claim for spousal maintenance, if applicable, including but not limited to the following:

Length of the marriage;

Standard of living established during the marriage;

Needs, obligations, and financial resources of the parties;

Age and physical and emotional condition of each party and each minor dependent child of the parties;

Extraordinary medical expenses for any minor dependent child;

Any circumstances making it appropriate that a party not seek employment outside of the home;

Contributions, monetary or otherwise, each party has made to the well-being of the family;

Property interests of each party, whether real or personal, tangible or intangible;

Education and training of each party;

Earning capacity and present employment opportunities of each party;

The extent to which each party had contributed to the attainment of education, training, or profession of the other party; and,

Any documentation relating to your claim that no spousal support should be ordered, if applicable.

23. Any and all documentation relating to your claim for child support, if applicable, including but not limited to the following:

> Monetary support for other family members, including but not limited to parents of the parties and children of one of the parties resulting from other relationships;
> Work-related child care for any of your dependent minor children for the past <u>36</u> months;
> Debts of either party incurred for the benefit of the children;
> Age and physical and emotional condition of each of the children;
> Any prior written agreements between the parties relating to the allocation of liability for the support of the children;
> Tax consequences to each party;
> Financial resources of any of the children;
> Standard of living for the family established during the marriage;
> Contributions, monetary or otherwise, each party has made to the well-being of the family;
> Education and training of each party; and,
> Earning capacity and present employment opportunities of each party.

24. Any and all documentation relating to your claim for distribution of marital property, if applicable, including but not limited to the following:

> Length of the marriage;
> Contributions, monetary or otherwise, each party has made to the well-being of the family;
> Age and physical and emotional condition of each of the children;
> Debts of each party, including the property serving as security for any secured debt;
> Tax consequences to each party;
> Circumstances contributing to the dissolution of the marriage;
> Evidence supporting your claim that any property is separate rather than marital property, if applicable; and,
> Evidence supporting your claim that any property claimed by your spouse is marital rather than separate property, if applicable.

25. Any and all documentation relating to your claim for custody of your dependent minor child(ren), if applicable, including but not limited to the following:

> Age and physical and emotional condition of each of the parties and of each child;

Needs of each child;

Relationship between each party with each child;

Documentation supporting your claim that you should be primary physical or legal custodian of your dependent minor children;

Likelihood of each parent to facilitate the children's relationship with the other parent;

Preference of each child of reasonable age and understanding to express such a preference;

History of abuse by either party of any child;

All documentation relating to the children's health care;

All documentation relating to day care providers used in the last <u>36</u> months;

All documentation relating to the education of each of the dependent minor children; and,

All documentation relating to the extracurricular activities of each of the dependent minor children.

26. Any and all documentation relating to the opinions of any experts you plan to call at trial, including but not limited to:

Any final report prepared by such expert and

Curriculum Vitae for each expert.

27. Any and all documentation supporting the allegations made in your pleadings.

28. Any and all documentation supporting your denials of the allegations made in the other party's pleadings.

29. Any and all documentation referenced by you in your Answers to Interrogatories.

Respectfully submitted,

*__Samuel Spouse__*_____

Signature

Name <u>George Repp</u>_____

Attorney for <u>Petitioner</u>_____

Address <u>567 Business Drive</u>_____

City, State, Zip <u>Springfield, ED 60600</u>___

Phone <u>(101) 555-4567</u>_____

IN THE DISTRICT COURT OF THE <u>FIRST</u> JUDICIAL DISTRICT STATE OF <u>EAST DAKOTA</u>

In Re the Marriage of:)
)
<u> Samuel Spouse   </u>)
          Petitioner,)
)   CASE NO. <u>2007D1234</u>
and   )
)
<u> Susan Spouse   </u>)
         Respondent.)

RESPONDENT'S RESPONSE TO PETITIONER'S REQUEST FOR PRODUCTION

<u>Susan Spouse</u>, Respondent in the captioned matter, hereby tenders the following in Response to Petitioner's Request for Production:

1. Any and all of your paycheck stubs from all employers for the past <u>36</u> months.
   <u>NA</u>

2. Any and all of your monthly retirement account statements from all employers for the past <u>36</u> months.
   <u>NA</u>

3. Any and all statements relating to any pension, profit-sharing, employee stock ownership, stock option, or deferred compensation plan owned by you, whether vested or unvested, for the past <u>36</u> months.
   <u>NA</u>

4. Any and all documentation relating to any health plan to which you belong, including any and all statements showing premiums paid by

you and/or benefits paid to you, whether for your own or any of your dependents' health care for the past <u>36</u> months.

> <u>Respondent belongs to Petitioner's health care plan; documents are in his possession and control</u>

5. If applicable, any and all statements relating to military retirement pay paid or owed to you, for the past <u>36</u> months.

> <u>NA</u>

6. Any and all documentation relating to any of the following for which you received any income for the past <u>36</u> months:
Social Security payments
Disability payments
Pension payments
Dividends
Patents
Trademarks
Copyrights
Royalties
Franchises
Trusts
Investments
Rents

> <u>NA for all</u>

7. Any and all documentation relating to any prizes, awards, gifts, rewards, or inheritances, valued at an amount greater than $500, received by you in the past <u>36</u> months.

> <u>NA</u>

8. Any and all documentation relating to any transfer, including transfer by sale, lease, abandonment, or gift, of any property in which you or your spouse, whether individually, jointly, or with any third party or parties, have or had any interest, which transfer took place at any time in the past <u>36</u> months.

> <u>NA</u>

9. Any and all documentation relating to any outstanding debts or accounts receivable owed to you or your spouse, whether individually, jointly, or with any third party or parties, for the past <u>36</u> months.
   <u>NA</u>

10. Statements for any and all checking, savings, credit union, and money market accounts, as well as certificates of deposit, which are held either in your name or your spouse's name, whether individually, jointly, or with any third party or parties, for the past <u>36</u> months.
    <u>See attached; Petitioner has control and custody of any statements pertaining to accounts within his name alone</u>

11. Statements for any and all mutual funds, stocks, bonds, other securities, IRA accounts, KEOGH accounts, 401(K) accounts, or other investment funds, which are held either in your name or your spouse's name, whether individually, jointly, or with any third party or parties, for the past <u>36</u> months.
    <u>See attached; Petitioner has control and custody of any statements pertaining to accounts within his name alone</u>

12. Any and all state and federal income tax returns, including all schedules, W-2 forms, and other attachments, for the calendar years <u>2002-2007</u>.
    <u>See attached</u>

13. Any and all appraisals or assessments for all personal property in which you and/or your spouse own any interest.
    <u>NA</u>

14. Any and all deeds, mortgages, promissory notes, tax bills, property tax assessments, appraisals, HUD-1 or other settlement statements, federal income mortgage interest statements for all real property in which you and/or your spouse own any interest or have owned any interest for the past <u>36</u> months.
    <u>Petitioner has all documentation related to marital home, in which he continues to live.</u>

15. Any and all life insurance policies or documentation reflecting the cash value of any such policies in which you or your spouse have had any interest in the past <u>36</u> months.
    <u>NA</u>

16. Any and all of your credit reports or histories you have received in the past <u>36</u> months.
    <u>NA</u>

17. Any and all credit card statements for all charge accounts held in your name, whether individually or jointly, for the past <u>36</u> months.
    <u>See attached</u>

18. Any and all documentation relating to any other indebtedness owed by you as of the date of service of this Request for Production.
    <u>Petitioner has in his possession and control all documentation regarding vehicles we own.</u>

19. Any and all state and federal income tax returns for any business, corporation, or partnership in which you are a partner, owner, or shareholder of more than a 5% interest, including all schedules and attachments, for the calendar years <u>2002–2007</u>.
    <u>NA</u>

20. Any and all documentation of receipts and disbursements, including accounts receivable and accounts payable ledgers, for any business, corporation, or partnership in which you are a partner, owner, or shareholder of more than a 5% interest, for the calendar years <u>2002–2007</u>.
    <u>NA</u>

21. For any business, corporation, or partnership in which you are a partner, owner, or shareholder of more than a 5% interest, any and all of the following documentation:
    Articles of incorporation and by-laws;

Partnership agreements;

Loan applications;

Financial statements;

Appraisals or assessments for all personal property owned by such business entity;

Deeds, mortgages, promissory notes, tax bills, property tax assessments, appraisals, HUD-1 or other settlement statements, federal income mortgage interest statements for all real property owned by such business entity;

Stock certificates;

Shareholder agreements;

Documents relating to your or your spouse's use of or entitlement to use of any business expense account, including but not limited to reimbursement for travel, lodging, or other personal living expenses; and,

Documents relating to your or spouse's use of or entitlement to use of any business loans; life, health, or other insurance; stock ownership, stock options or stock bonuses; profit-sharing, or any other employee benefit plans for any business, corporation, or partnership in which you are a partner, owner, or shareholder of more than a five percent interest.

    <u>NA</u>

22. Any and all documentation relating to your claim for spousal maintenance, if applicable, including but not limited to the following:

Length of the marriage;

Standard of living established during the marriage;

Needs, obligations, and financial resources of the parties;

Age and physical and emotional condition of each party and each minor dependent child of the parties;

Extraordinary medical expenses for any minor dependent child;

Any circumstances making it appropriate that a party not seek employment outside of the home;

Contributions, monetary or otherwise, each party has made to the well-being of the family;

Property interests of each party, whether real or personal, tangible or intangible;

Education and training of each party;

Earning capacity and present employment opportunities of each party;

The extent to which each party had contributed to the attainment of education, training, or profession of the other party; and,

Any documentation relating to your claim that no spousal support should be ordered, if applicable.

See attached copy of marriage license and college diploma

23. Any and all documentation relating to your claim for child support, if applicable, including but not limited to the following:

Monetary support for other family members, including but not limited to parents of the parties and children of one of the parties resulting from other relationships;

Work-related child care for any of your dependent minor children for the past 36 months;

Debts of either party incurred for the benefit of the children;

Age and physical and emotional condition of each of the children;

Any prior written agreements between the parties relating to the allocation of liability for the support of the children;

Tax consequences to each party;

Financial resources of any of the children;

Standard of living for the family established during the marriage;

Contributions, monetary or otherwise, each party has made to the well-being of the family;

Education and training of each party; and,

Earning capacity and present employment opportunities of each party.

See attached documentation relating to standard of living; i.e. credit card statements from last five years showing living expenses for family

24. Any and all documentation relating to your claim for distribution of marital property, if applicable, including but not limited to the following:

Length of the marriage;

Contributions, monetary or otherwise, each party has made to the well-being of the family;

Age and physical and emotional condition of each of the children;

Debts of each party, including the property serving as security for any secured debt;

Tax consequences to each party;

Circumstances contributing to the dissolution of the marriage;

Evidence supporting your claim that any property is separate rather than marital property, if applicable; and,

Evidence supporting your claim that any property claimed by your spouse is marital rather than separate property, if applicable.

See attached copies of emails from Petitioner to his office assistant

25. Any and all documentation relating to your claim for custody of your dependent minor child(ren), if applicable, including but not limited to the following:

Age and physical and emotional condition of each of the parties and of each child;

Needs of each child;

Relationship between each party with each child;

Documentation supporting your claim that you should be primary physical or legal custodian of your dependent minor children;

Likelihood of each parent to facilitate the children's relationship with the other parent;

Preference of each child of reasonable age and understanding to express such a preference;

History of abuse by either party of any child;

All documentation relating to the children's health care;

All documentation relating to day care providers used in the last 36 months;

All documentation relating to the education of each of the dependent minor children; and,

All documentation relating to the extracurricular activities of each of the dependent minor children.

NA

26. Any and all documentation relating to the opinions of any experts you plan to call at trial, including but not limited to:

Any final report prepared by such expert and

Curriculum Vitae for each expert.

<u>NA</u>

27. Any and all documentation supporting the allegations made in your pleadings.

<u>NA</u>

28. Any and all documentation supporting your denials of the allegations made in the other party's pleadings.

<u>NA</u>

29. Any and all documentation referenced by you in your Answers to Interrogatories.

<u>NA</u>

Respectfully submitted,

<u>**Susan Spouse**</u>

Signature

Name <u>Lawrence Lawyer</u>

Attorney for <u>Respondent</u>

Address <u>456 State Street</u>

City, State, Zip <u>Dakota City, ED 60600</u>

Phone <u>(101) 555-7654</u>

IN THE DISTRICT COURT OF THE <u>FIRST</u> JUDICIAL DISTRICT
STATE OF <u>EAST DAKOTA</u>

In Re the Marriage of:)
)
<u> Samuel Spouse   </u>   )
                      Petitioner,   )
)   CASE NO. <u>2007D1234</u>
and   )
)
<u> Susan Spouse   </u>   )
                      Respondent.   )

PETITION FOR DECLARATION OF INVALIDITY OF MARRIAGE

<u>Samuel Spouse</u>, Petitioner in this case, having been duly sworn, hereby states as follows:

1. (Check only one) ___Petitioner ___Respondent <u>X</u> Both have resided in the State of <u>East Dakota</u> for more than 30 days prior to the filing of this action.
2. The marriage between Petitioner and Respondent was entered into in the State of <u>East Dakota</u>, on <u>November 1, 1988</u>.
3. The marriage is registered in <u>Springfield County, East Dakota</u>.
4. Petitioner states that the marriage is invalid and void ab initio because:<u>   the marriage was prohibited by statute </u>
(state statutory grounds for declaration of invalidity)

5. The Petitioner and Respondent are both the parents of the following dependent children:

Name <u>Sarah Spouse   </u> DOB <u> 2/3/96 </u> Age <u>11 </u>
Name <u> Sean Spouse   </u> DOB <u> 5/11/00 </u> Age <u>6   </u>

6. Respondent is not pregnant at this time.
7. Child Custody *If the parties have no dependent children, skip section 7.* Have the parties agreed to child custody and/or visitation in a written agreement? (check one) ___Yes <u>x</u> No *If Yes, attach written agreement to Petition; if no, complete sections 7.a., 7.b., and 7.c. below.*

a. Legal custody (check only one)

    <u>x</u> It is in the child(ren)'s best interest that legal custody be shared by both parties.

    ___It is in the child(ren)'s best interest that legal custody be awarded solely to (check one) ___Petitioner ___Respondent, because

    _____.

b. Physical custody (check only one)

    <u>x</u> It is in the child(ren)'s best interest that physical custody be shared by both parties.

    ___It is in the child(ren)'s best interest that physical custody be awarded solely to
(check one)___Petitioner ___Respondent, because _____

    _____.

c. Visitation (check only one)

    ___It is in the child(ren)'s best interest that the Court provide for parental visitation as follows: _____
_____

    ___It is in the child(ren)'s best interest that the Court (check one)
___deny
___restrict visitation, because _____
_____

8. Child Support *If the parties have no dependent children, skip section 8.* (check all that apply)

    <u>x</u> Petitioner requests the Court award child support pursuant to the State of <u>East Dakota</u> Child Support Guidelines, with such support retroactive to <u>March 1, 2007</u> (date).

    ___Petitioner requests that the Court order support to be paid beyond the age of 18 years because _____
_____

    ___ Petitioner requests that the Court award child support in an amount that is more or less than the State of <u>East Dakota</u> Child Support Guidelines, because

    _____
_____

    ___ Petitioner requests that (check only one) <u>x</u> Petitioner
___ Respondent be ordered to provide medical and dental insurance coverage for the dependent minor child(ren).

    ___ Petitioner requests that (check only one) ___Petitioner ___

Respondent __x_ both be ordered to pay all uninsured medical and dental expenses for the dependent minor child(ren).

___Petitioner requests that life insurance to secure child support be provided by (check only one) ___Petitioner ___Respondent _x_ both.

WHEREFORE, Petitioner respectfully requests this Honorable Court to:

Declare the marriage between the parties invalid and void ab initio;

Declare the dependent minor children of the marriage to be legitimate and to grant custody of said children as requested in the Petition;

Grant child support as requested in the Petition; and,

Order such further relief as the Court deems necessary and proper.

Dated: _4/1/07_   *Samuel Spouse*_____
                                 Signature of Petitioner

                                 Samuel Spouse_____
                                 Print or Type Name

I declare under penalty of perjury under the laws of the State of East Dakota that the foregoing is true and correct.
Signed at Springfield, East Dakota on April 1, 2007.

_**Samuel Spouse**_____   Samuel Spouse_____
Signature of Petitioner   Print or Type Name

SWORN TO AND subscribed before me in the County of Springfield, on April 1, 2007.

_Nancy Notary_____
NOTARY PUBLIC

My Commission Expires: notary seal
June 1, 2007

IN THE DISTRICT COURT OF THE <u>FIRST</u> JUDICIAL DISTRICT
STATE OF <u>EAST DAKOTA</u>

In Re the Marriage of:　　　　　　)
　　　　　　　　　　　　　　　　)
　<u>Samuel Spouse</u>　　　　　　)
　　　　　　　　　Petitioner,　　)
　　　　　　　　　　　　　　　　)　　CASE NO. <u>2007D1234</u>
and　　　　　　　　　　　　　　)
　　　　　　　　　　　　　　　　)
　<u>Susan Spouse</u>　　　　　　　)
　　　　　　　　　Respondent.　)

AFFIDAVIT OF NO MILITARY SERVICE

<u>Samuel Spouse</u>, Petitioner and Affiant herein, being duly sworn, hereby states as follows:

1. I know of my own personal knowledge that the Respondent is not in the United States Armed Forces, because (check all that apply):
   <u>x</u> I know the Respondent personally and know that he is not a member of the United States Military or National Guard.
   ___Respondent contacted me on _____(date) and told me personally that he/she is not a member of the United States Military or National Guard.
   ___I am in regular contact with Respondent and do not believe that he/she is on active duty at this time.
   ___Other: _____.
2. I have inquired of the United States Armed Forces to determine whether Respondent is a member of the military and am attaching a certificate stating that Respondent is not now in the Armed Forces.

Dated: <u>June 1, 2007</u>   ***Samuel Spouse***
                                              Signature of Petitioner

                                                Samuel Spouse
                                                Print or Type Name

I declare under penalty of perjury under the laws of the State of <u>East Dakota</u> that the foregoing is true and correct.

Signed at <u>Springfield</u>, <u>East Dakota</u> on <u>June 1, 2007</u>.

Samuel Spouse   Samuel Spouse
Signature of Petitioner   Print or Type Name

SWORN TO AND subscribed before me in the County of <u>Springfield</u>, on <u>June 1, 2007</u>.

    Nancy Notary
NOTARY PUBLIC

My Commission Expires: notary seal
<u>November 1, 2007</u>

IN THE DISTRICT COURT OF THE <u>FIRST</u> JUDICIAL DISTRICT STATE OF <u>EAST DAKOTA</u>

In Re the Marriage of:)
)
<u> Samuel Spouse   </u>)
 Petitioner,)
) CASE NO. <u>2007D1234</u>
and)
)
<u> Susan Spouse   </u>)
 Respondent.)

NOTICE OF MOTION

TO: <u>Lawrence Lawyer</u>
<u>Attorney at Law</u>
<u>456 State Street</u>
<u>Dakota City, ED 60600</u>

On <u>June 1, 2007</u>, at <u>9:00 </u>a.m.~~/p.m.~~, or as soon thereafter as Counsel may be heard, I shall appear before the Honorable <u>Julia Jurist</u>, or any judge sitting in his/her stead, in the courtroom usually occupied by him/her in the <u>Dakota County Government Center, 789 Eighth Street, Dakota City,</u> <u>East Dakota</u>, and then and there present the following Motion:

PETITIONER'S MOTION TO APPOINT GUARDIAN AD LITEM

at which time and place you may appear and respond if you so desire.

<u>*George Repp*   </u>
Attorney's Signature

Name <u> George Repp   </u>
Attorney for <u>Petitioner   </u>
Address <u> 567 Business Drive   </u>
City, State, Zip <u>Springfield, ED   </u>
Phone <u>(101) 555-4567   </u>

IN THE DISTRICT COURT OF THE <u>FIRST</u> JUDICIAL DISTRICT STATE OF <u>EAST DAKOTA</u>

In Re the Marriage of:

<u> Samuel Spouse </u>

                  Petitioner,

and

<u> Susan Spouse </u>

              Respondent.

CASE NO. <u>2007D1234</u>

PROOF OF SERVICE

<u>Lawrence Lawyer</u>
<u>456 State Street</u>
<u>Dakota City, ED 60600</u>

The undersigned, being first duly sworn on oath deposes and says that a copy of the foregoing Notice was served upon the above named by enclosing the same in an envelope, plainly addressed as is shown above, postage fully prepaid, and by depositing the same in a United States Post Office Box, at <u>Springfield, East Dakota</u>, on the <u>15th</u> day of <u>May, 2007</u>, before the hour of 4:00 p.m.

<u>George Repp</u>
Signature

SUBSCRIBED and SWORN to before me this
<u>15th</u> day of <u>May, 2007</u>.

<u>   *Nancy Notary*   </u>
NOTARY PUBLIC   notary seal

MY COMMISSION EXPIRES:
<u>November 1, 2007</u>

IN THE DISTRICT COURT OF THE <u>FIRST</u> JUDICIAL DISTRICT STATE OF <u>EAST DAKOTA</u>

In Re the Marriage of:)
)
<u> Samuel Spouse   </u>)
                  Petitioner,)
) CASE NO. <u>2007D1234</u>
and)
)
<u> Susan Spouse   </u>)
              Respondent.)

MARITAL SETTLEMENT AGREEMENT

NOW COME the Petitioner, <u>Samuel Spouse</u>, and the Respondent, <u>Susan Spouse</u>, and for their Marital Settlement Agreement, entered into on <u>May 15, 2007</u> state as follows:

I. PARTIES' INFORMATION

1. The parties were married on the <u>1st</u> day of <u>November, 1988</u> in <u>Dakota City</u>, county of <u>Springfield</u>, <u>East Dakota</u>.
2. The parties have resided in <u>East Dakota</u> since <u>November, 1988</u>.
3. The following children were born to or adopted by the parties, and the Wife is not now pregnant.

NAME	DATE OF BIRTH
<u>Sarah Spouse </u>	<u>2/3/96 </u>
<u>Sean Spouse </u>	<u>5/11/00 </u>

4. The parties wish to obtain a dissolution of their marriage, due to the irretrievable breakdown of their marriage.

5. The parties have lived separately for the past <u>12 months</u>.

6. The parties enter into this agreement without any force, fraud, or duress, each having been represented by counsel. The parties' objective is to terminate the marriage, and each believes it to be the best interests of both parties and of the parties' children to enter this agreement settling any and all matters arising pursuant to the dissolution of the marriage. These matters include but are not limited to maintenance, property division and debt allocation, child custody, and child support.

II. MAINTENANCE

7. The parties hereby agree to waive any and all rights to maintenance that either may have claimed against the other.

III. PROPERTY DIVISION AND DEBT ALLOCATION

8. Each party shall retain any and all personal property in the party's possession as his or her separate property. All remaining property has been divided between the parties prior to this agreement. Each party hereby waives any claim to any property distributed by this agreement to the other party.

9. Each party shall be responsible for debts as follows:

<u>Husband: car loan with Turbostar Auto Finance Co., principal amount $10,097, account no. 76947</u>

<u>Wife: mortgage on residence with First National Bank of Dakota, principal amount $159,245, account no. 990998</u>

Each party shall hold the other harmless for any debt for which the party has agreed to be responsible according to this agreement.

IV. CHILD CUSTODY AND VISITATION

10. The parties agree that they shall have joint custody of the minor children of the marriage. <u>Wife</u> shall have primary physical custody of the minor children; <u>Husband</u> shall have reasonable and liberal visitation with the minor children, subject to review by the Court at any time either party believes such review is necessary and proper. <u>Husband</u>'s visitation shall be as follows:

    <u>Husband shall have children from 6:00 p.m. every Wednesday until 8:00 a.m. the following day; every other weekend, from 6:00 p.m. Friday until 6:00 p.m. Sunday; every Father's Day and Husband's birthday; and alternating on the following holidays: Easter, Thanksgiving, Christmas Eve, and Christmas. On the first holidays occurring after Court approval of this agreement, Wife shall have the children on Easter and Christmas, and Husband shall have the children on Thanksgiving and Christmas Eve, then both shall alternate the same holidays each year thereafter.</u>

V. CHILD SUPPORT

11. <u>Husband</u> shall pay <u>Wife</u>, directly and without withholding by the State of <u>East Dakota</u>, the amount of <u>$600</u> per month on behalf of the minor children, for their support, to be reduced by <u>one-half</u> upon the emancipation or death of each child, whichever comes first, and to be terminated altogether upon the emancipation or death of the youngest child, whichever comes first.

12. <u>Husband</u> shall maintain health and dental insurance for the minor children. Husband and Wife agree to pay equally for all uninsured medical expenses for the minor children.

13. Husband and Wife agree to claim the minor children as dependents, for tax purposes, on alternating tax years. <u>Husband</u> shall be allowed

to claim the minor children as dependents on the tax return that is due for the tax year during which this agreement is approved by the Court.

VI. MISCELLANEOUS

14. Each party shall be responsible for payment of attorney's fees to his or her own counsel.

15. The parties agree that Wife shall be entitled to return to the use of her maiden name, as soon as the marriage is ordered dissolved.

Samuel Spouse   *May 15, 2007*
Signature of Party   Date

Susan Spouse   *May 15, 2007*
Signature of Party   Date

SUBSCRIBED and SWORN to before me this
15th day of May, 2007.

Nancy Notary
NOTARY PUBLIC   notary seal

MY COMMISSION EXPIRES:
November 1, 2007

IN THE DISTRICT COURT OF THE <u>FIRST</u> JUDICIAL DISTRICT
STATE OF <u>EAST DAKOTA</u>

In Re the Marriage of:)
)

<u> Samuel Spouse   </u>   )
               Petitioner,   )

and   )   CASE NO. <u>2007D1234</u>

<u> Susan Spouse   </u>)
               Respondent.)

PETITION TO MODIFY CUSTODY

NOW COMES the Petitioner, <u>Samuel Spouse</u>, by and through his attorney, <u>George Repp</u>, and in support of his Petition to Modify Custody, states as follows:

1. Petitioner resides in <u>Springfield County, East Dakota</u>.

2. Respondent, <u>Susan Spouse</u>, resides in <u>Springfield County, East Dakota</u>.

3. Petitioner and Respondent are the parents of the following minor children:
Name <u> Sarah Spouse   </u> DOB <u> 2/3/96 </u> Age <u>11 </u>
Name <u> Sean Spouse   </u> DOB <u> 5/11/00 </u> Age <u>6   </u>

4. On September 1, 2007, this Court entered its order granting legal and physical custody of the above-named children to Respondent.

5. The above-named children currently reside with Respondent in <u>Springfield County, East Dakota</u>.

6. Since the date of the previous order regarding custody, there has been a substantial change in circumstances in this matter, in that <u>Respondent has developed a substance abuse problem that has caused her employer to terminate her employment, and in that the substance abuse remains untreated</u>.

7. It is in the best interest of the children that the Court's previous order be modified to grant legal and physical custody of the children to <u>Petitioner</u>.

8. More than two years have passed since the entry of the previous order regarding custody.

WHEREFORE, Petitioner requests that this Honorable Court modify its earlier custody order, such that Petitioner be granted immediate legal and physical custody of the above-named minor children.

Samuel Spouse
Petitioner

Name __George Repp_____
Attorney for <u>Petitioner</u>_____
Address _567 Business Drive_____
City, State, Zip <u>Springfield, ED, 60600</u>
Phone <u>(101) 555-4567</u>_____

STATE OF __EAST DAKOTA____)
)
COUNTY OF _SPRINGFIELD____)

_Samuel Spouse_____, being first duly sworn on oath, deposes and states that he has read the foregoing document, and the answers made herein are true, correct and complete to the best of his knowledge and belief.

_*Samuel Spouse*_____
SIGNATURE

SUBSCRIBED and SWORN to before me this _1st_ day of __April, 2009_.

_*Nancy Notary*_____
NOTARY PUBLIC   notary seal

MY COMMISSION EXPIRES:
June 1, 2009

Index

About the Author

Linda H. Connell received her law degree from Notre Dame Law School. She has served as an arbitrator for the Circuit Court in DuPage County, Illinois and in general practice, has worked in the area of domestic relations. Ms. Connell is licensed to practice law in Nevada, Colorado, and Illinois. She currently lives in the Chicago area.